T0065731

Also by Harry S. Dent, Jr.

THE ROARING 2000s:
   Building the Lifestyle You Desire in the
   Greatest Boom in History
THE GREAT BOOM AHEAD:
   Your Comprehensive Guide to Personal
   and Business Profit
   in the New Age of Prosperity

THE

Roaring 2000s Investor

Strategies for the Life You Want

Harry S. Dent, Jr.

A Touchstone Book
Published by Simon & Schuster
New York   London   Toronto   Sydney   Singapore

To Richard Nuttall,
my first mentor in investments

TOUCHSTONE
Rockefeller Center
1230 Avenue of the Americas
New York, NY 10020

Copyright © 1999 by Harry S. Dent, Jr.

First Touchstone Edition 2000
TOUCHSTONE and colophon are
registered trademarks of Simon & Schuster, Inc.

Designed by Edith Fowler

Manufactured in the United States of America

10 9 8 7 6 5 4 3 2

The Library of Congress has cataloged the Simon & Schuster edition
as follows:

Dent, Harry S., Jr.
   The roaring 2000s investor : strategies for the life you want / Harry S.
Dent, Jr.
        p.   cm.
   Includes index.
      1. Investments—United States.   2. Economic forecasting—United
States.   3. United States—Economic conditions—1981–   I. Title.
II. Title: The Roaring 2000s Investor.
HG4910.D46   1999
332.6—dc21   99-43185
                                                                          CIP

ISBN 0-684-86232-8
      0-684-86231-X (Pbk)

Acknowledgments

Thanks to my literary agent, Susan Golomb; my marketing agent, Harry Cornelius; my research and investment director, George May; my executive assistant, Eva Sturm-Kehoe; my accountant, Donna Windell; my graphic artist, Martie Sautter; and in sales, Mark Gonsalves and Greg Blood. Special thanks to the founding members of the H. S. Dent Advisory Network: Bill Gold, Alan and Beth Blecker, Floyd and Rosa Shilanski, Joe Clark, Bill and Phyllis Nelson, Steve Takeda, and Michael Robertson.

Contents

Foreword: The Markets Roar On...
After the Correction of 2000

WHEN *THE ROARING 2000S INVESTOR* was originally published in the fall of 1999, I was projecting a Dow as high as 35,000 to 41,000 by 2008. These forecasts were predicated upon the very predictable spending and productivity cycle of the massive baby boom generation that is not due to peak until around mid-2009. After the greatest market correction since 1987, many people may now be questioning my very bullish predictions. But people who understand my forecasting methods will not be surprised to learn that I have not changed my long-term forecasts. Demographics simply project quantifiable human behaviors into the future as people age. Hence, the long-term direction and level of trends are not affected by the many short-term political, psychological, and random events that can affect the market in the short term. That is the advantage to investors. You can see the most important trends that will affect your investments over the rest of your lifetime.

The correction of 2000 was not a surprise nor was it a contradiction to the long-term trends I have been forecasting. I warned on page 26 of this book that the valuation boom in price/earnings ratios on stocks that had surged since 1995 would come to an end by late 1999 to mid-2000. The markets did indeed hit a peak in valuations in early 2000 and experienced a strong correction into mid-2000. The Dow corrected about 20 percent into early March, testing the midpoint or fair value trend-line in the Dow channel on page 27, Chart 1-2. That was to be expected after the first time the Dow hit the top of the channel since 1987. But the real correction came in the Nasdaq, which followed with a correction of almost 40 percent into late May. Given the extreme in valuations on technology stocks, that should not have been a big surprise. And as of June 1, when this foreword was written, it appears the Nasdaq could correct further in this unprecedented bull market.

Was this a bubble in Internet and tech stocks that signaled an end to their incredible gains for investors? Here again my forecasts remain unchanged. In *The Roaring 2000s* (1998) I show how computers are accelerating into the mainstream economy from 1994 into 2008 just as cars did from 1914 to 1928 during the last technology revolution. That not only means a surge in productivity that will bolster the economy and stock market but it also means that technology will be the strongest segment of the economy from the mid-1990s into the top of this boom. What is occurring for the Nasdaq is an extreme correction similar to what the Dow and broader markets experienced in 1987. The correction of 2000 will create the best buying opportunity in the most promising investment sector for the coming decade.

The Nasdaq only started to hit a more powerful growth trend in the early to mid-nineties consistent with this acceleration into the mainstream. The extreme peak and correction allowed me finally to plot a long-term channel of growth with high and low valuation extremes as I have done with the Dow in this book. As you can see in the following chart, we could see the Nasdaq as high as 25,000 by 2008. That is eight times the level of the Nasdaq on June 1, 2000, which means that technology stocks should still greatly outperform the broader market.

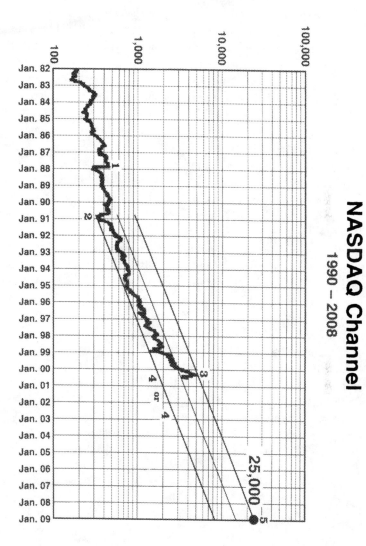

NASDAQ Channel
1990 — 2008

The Dow has been growing at a long-term rate of around 16 percent since 1982 with a volatility range of 20 percent above that trend on the upside and 20 percent below on the downside. This Nasdaq channel is growing at about 20 percent per year, but with volatility rates of 30 percent above or below. Although the Nasdaq is growing 20 percent faster than the Dow, the volatility levels are 50 percent higher. Hence, **the Nasdaq is no bargain when adjusted for risk!** You are very likely to continue to get the highest returns in technology stocks and mutual funds, but the risk of being in that one sector alone is excessive for most investors. As of June 1, the Nasdaq had made several attempts to put in a bottom and rally, but all had failed. There is a good chance that the correction could extend well into the lower half of the channel as the Dow did in 1987. If that were to occur, the Nasdaq could fall as low as 2,000, which is more than a 60 percent fall from the top of 5,132. Such a correction, if it occurred, would cause most investors to sell at the wrong time and to sour on tech stocks just when they were the best buy in decades. If you can buy nearer the bottom of this channel, your returns will average much higher than the average growth rates projected.

I have an alternate Nasdaq channel projecting as high as 30,000 with a 23 percent growth rate. That means growth in returns 45 percent higher than the Dow. Also note that the correction of 2000 has tended to confirm the 35,000 Dow channel in *The Roaring 2000s* (Figure 12.4, page 294) vs. the 41,000 Dow channel in this book. But that is just the difference between a 16 percent annual growth rate vs. 17 percent. Either way I continue to see technology as the strongest sector for investing, followed by financial services, health care, and Asia. This book will show you how to diversify effectively within these outperforming sectors to beat the S&P 500 at lower risks.

Also note that the technology sector has grown to become a larger percentage of the S&P 500 since the back-testing for optimal portfolios was done over the last decade. Hence, I am recommending increasing the weightings for technology in all of the portfolios in Chapter 2. The most popular "aggressive portfolio" in Chart 2-1 on page 58 should be weighted 40 percent technology, 30 percent financial services, 15 percent health care, and 20 percent Asia (ex-Japan). As a general rule I would up the technology weightings in all portfolios

25 percent to 30 percent. The attractive valuations created by this correction give only more reason to do so at this time.

The correction of 2000 has demonstrated why I recommend in this book that investors diversify their portfolios into other demographically leveraged sectors, such as financial services, health care, and Asia (ex-Japan). Many investors will also understand why I recommend systematic investing as opposed to the rampant trend toward day-trading. And you are now more likely to understand why I recommend working with a competent, objective financial advisor.

Take the time to carefully understand the simple but powerful tools for forecasting and investing that are presented in this book. Your quality of life in the future will depend on it and should benefit substantially. Stay with this powerful bull market. Best of success to you!

Introduction: Fitting Your Lifestyle and Investments to the Seasons of the Economy

IN THE ROARING 2000s, I forecast a new era of prosperity even greater than the "Roaring '20s." The purpose of this book is to help you develop very specific investment stategies to leverage this unprecedented boom so that you can have the freedom to create the life you most want. Despite forecasting a Dow as high as 35,000 by 2008, I also forecast on page 292 of *The Roaring 2000s* that the Dow would correct to the 7200 to 7600 range between May and November of 1998. The low close was 7539 on August 30, 1998. Now, as the Dow has made new highs in 1999, we are seeing a vindication of the very fundamentals of baby boom earning and spending that I have been forecasting since 1988 in previous books, from *Our Power to Predict* (1989) to *The Great Boom Ahead* (1993) to *The Great Jobs Ahead* (1995).

The secret to building wealth is to understand such fundamental trends and stay invested in the sustained bull markets they create! Now that more investors are recognizing the power of the most important technological and population trends since the emergence of the printing press, the key to investment profits will come from:

- Recognizing which sectors of our economy will benefit from predictable demographic and technological trends.
- Learning the most essential principles of investing exhibited by the

best investors, from Benjamin Graham to Peter Lynch to Warren
Buffet.

- Choosing a financial advisor who can be your objective browser and
representative, optimizing not only your investment returns but also
your credit, tax, insurance, and estate planning needs. Or designing
a systematic approach to investment yourself if you have the time
and discipline.

In this book I will show why the most cherished principles of investment for achieving the greatest returns at the lowest risks are substantially flawed and why each predictable phase of this economic
revolution should generate very different investment and portfolio
strategies. How do you beat the S&P 500 and increasingly popular
index funds? With the best sectors of the S&P! Large company stocks
and international equities will outperform in the coming decade, as
they did in the Roaring '20s. Bonds and small cap stocks will underperform. Baby boomers will drive stellar performance in industries
like financial services, health care, home furnishings, and travel and
leisure. The technology revolution will favor those stocks, especially
the software and Internet-oriented companies. In real estate, vacation
and resort areas will shine, as will ex-urban areas outside the suburban
areas that flourished into the 1980s. And in the next global downturn,
bonds, select international investments (especially in Japan, China,
and South Korea), and small company stocks will excel.

**There is not one portfolio strategy that will serve you best over
your lifetime, any more than the same personal life strategy
would. You need to prosper in good times and bad and in inflationary and deflationary times.**

I will give specific recommendations for how to prosper in the
next global downturn as well as the great boom ahead. The global
scare from late 1997 into late 1998 was not it! We will see Asia and
Latin America and most areas of the world rebound strongly, with the
exception of Japan. I will look at the age demographics of most key
countries around the world and show how you can benefit from the
global resurgence. Many countries will continue to boom even after
the United States and many other countries falter after 2009. New in-

dustries will continue to emerge and old ones will stumble, and of course that is the same for companies. This is not the 1950s and 1960s, a tide that raises all boats. I will help you see where to invest in this era of dramatic domestic and global change.

You are being told that inflation will greatly increase everything from your kids' college costs to your retirement. This is not the trend! Inflation rates have been falling since 1980 and have been falling in health care even faster in the 1990s. Education costs will be the next to fall. The only rising costs will come from new choices and a rising quality of life that we should all welcome. In fact, we will enter a deflationary era after 2009 that will see falling costs in most areas just as baby boomers start to retire. This means more of our investment funds can go toward creating the lifestyle and retirement we really desire. That should be the focus of your planning today: how to create abundance, not how to cope with scarcity. Social Security funds will swell well beyond forecasts in the next decade but then will start to falter faster than forecast because of the inevitable downturn after 2009. How do you protect yourself when that finally occurs? I will give you specific investment strategies for offsetting that crisis.

Tax laws have been changing. Lower capital gains and home exemptions are great for investors. I will show how life-insurance-oriented or "variable annuity" investments can give you even greater tax-deferral benefits despite the campaign in the press against them that argues that the slightly higher costs of such policies offset the tax-deferral benefits. Those arguments assume much lower investment returns than are common in this boom. Higher investment returns like the ones I will propose will greatly favor tax-deferred investment strategies, especially for those in higher tax brackets. In fact, it is possible to pay no taxes on your investments and to have your excess returns go to charities that you value or pass to your heirs.

The key message of this book is that you can create the wealth and lifestyle you desire in the great boom ahead and, more important, in the great bust to follow. Decide what you want to do today, decide where you want to live today, and use the simple, proven principles in this book to take control of your own life.

Don't listen to people who say you can enhance your wealth by picking your own stocks over the Internet. You have better things to do, and there are better people to do that. Don't listen to people who say the world is about to come to an end because of the Y2K crisis. Remember the people who said that the Asian crisis would cause an extended recession in the United States? There will be problems from Y2K, but they will lead to greater innovations in this incredible technological revolution.

Don't listen to people who claim that you have to live a minimal life today to retire well tomorrow. You can spend what it takes to have a great life now if you focus on what really creates value for you, and still have enough to invest in this incredible stock market to provide for an enriching life tomorrow. Don't listen to the past generation that said we don't have moral values. Instead, create new personal, family, social, and political values that can generate the next leap in our standard of living and quality of life. Don't listen to those who say your kids won't have the same standard of living as you. Create the environment through new technologies that can create a leap in learning and communications capacities in our schools and at home.

Money is not a means in itself to merely show off your achievements. It represents the capacity to achieve the freedom to do what you want in life and to contribute to the evolution of our society. I will show you how to achieve wealth and financial freedom. You can decide what to do with that wealth. Baby boomers will predictably create a new ethic of retirement and contribution to society. It all comes down to understanding fundamental trends and the secrets of investing that the wealthy have always employed. Most of all, it doesn't mean living a life as boring as "the millionaire next door." Although you can choose that if you prefer. **But why not live and retire in style, however you define that!**

PART 1

Building Your Wealth
in Good Times
and Bad

CHAPTER 1
A Lifetime Planning and Investment Horizon Today

WHEN I FIRST PUBLISHED *The Great Boom Ahead* in late 1992, most experts and people felt the long-term prospects for our economic future were dim at best. *Bankruptcy 1995* was the bestselling book of the times. Similarly, I published *The Roaring 2000s* in early 1998 just as the markets were about to take their biggest correction since 1990 and the developing world was falling into a severe recession. I predicted a correction in the Dow to the 7200 to 7600 level by August to November of 1998 on page 292. In that book I was even more bullish, projecting a Dow as high as 35,000 by 2008. The astounding market rebound since early October 1998 has again vindicated the basic fundamentals driving our economy, the massive spending and productivity trends of the largest generation in world history, the baby boom. In this book I will look at the very specific investment strategies for leveraging the greatest boom in history that will see its grand crescendo in the next decade, especially from around late 2002 into 2008 or 2009. But your life and your investments will have to thrive beyond this great boom. I will show you how you can prosper in good times and in not-so-good times or even the worst of times. It all comes down to understanding long-term trends.

Let's face it. There have been many good books on investments and financial planning. But they all tend to focus on the same issues.

You need to save more and spend less. You need to have a long-term strategy and stick to a disciplined system of investing. You need to take advantage of tax-deductible and tax-deferred vehicles like your 401K. But everyone has heard this, and some of us practice this boring approach, while most investors continue to think they can beat the pros by selecting their own stocks, save commissions by trading over the Internet, and time the markets by listening to the best experts on TV. In fact, most studies show that the boring investors who stick to a systematic plan and use an objective financial advisor do much better. But what is the real secret to successful investing?

> **The secret to successful investing is understanding very fundamental long-term trends . . . and buying when companies and investments in those sectors are undervalued, when no one wants them. There are always investments that are booming, even in bad times. And we will see a very difficult economy after 2009.**

This is another popular topic in investment books, how you can use your own common sense to spot new trends. But can you really spot the next Wal-Mart in its early stages, as Peter Lynch did? Did you see the potential worldwide for Coca-Cola in the early 1980s, as Warren Buffet did when the market was getting saturated in the United States? Are you going to spot the next hot mutual fund or sector in the economy when it is down and unpopular? Or are you going to buy that mutual fund right when it is at the top of its cycle, with the highest ratings, and then watch it underperform and sell it before it starts singing again? Are you going to anticipate the next 10% or 20% correction in the stock market and get out right at the top and back in right at the bottom? Will you buy Japan 10 years from now, when it is booming again, after it has been a terrible investment for almost two decades? Will you buy bonds when the Dow is at something like 40,000, after bonds have yielded the lowest returns in decades?

So the real question is how do you understand long-term trends and how do you actually get on a systematic investment plan that keeps your emotions from working against you? Your emotions will always tell you to buy what is already hot or to avoid what has underperformed! How many of you trading on your own have beat the S&P 500 in the last 5 or 10 years? Forget how much fun you have investing—or gambling, as some would put it. Forget the ego trip of beating the pros on your own computer. The Beardstown ladies seemed to do this, until they were audited! They made 9%, not the 23% claimed, while the S&P gained 18%.

Are you willing to compromise the rest of your life and underperform the markets by as much as 4% to 10% (as studies have consistently shown) in this extraordinary boom? Do you know the price of that on your net worth and life and retirement options 20 to 40 years from now? The difference between 10% compounded annually, which most people tend to get, and the average 17% growth rate of the S&P 500 since 1982 over the next 10 years alone is 96.79%. And I will show how you could earn as much as 20% to 24% over the coming decade without taking substantially more risk than an index fund. How do you beat the S&P 500? By investing in the best sectors of the S&P 500, sectors that diversify each other and reduce the risks of investing! But you can't just pick the sectors that did the best in the past; that is a proven way to underperform the markets. You must understand what sectors will do well in the future, based on fundamental trends.

And what will you do when the stock markets in the United States start going down for many years, as they did from 1929 to 1942 and from 1968 to 1982? If you have been underperforming in this great boom, how will you do in the next great bust? Won't your emotions tell you that the stock market is the best bet when it has been going up for 26 to 27 years? That is when it goes down by past history.

> Here's the real truth: Life should be interesting; investment and financial planning should be boring. You should focus on what you enjoy and do best in life and let an objective financial advisor put you on a proven system for building the wealth that you deserve to achieve your life goals. Or you can set up such a system yourself if you have the discipline. But you can do that only if you understand the fundamental trends driving our economy.

In the greatest boom in history, you should be able to live an enjoyable lifestyle and plan adequately for your future. I don't think that *The Millionaire Next Door* necessarily represents the guide to your best strategy for the future. It was an enlightening book precisely because it showed how not to enjoy life from being successful. The typical millionaire profiled got rich by saving money and having a very boring life that entailed constant scrimping and doing everything himself or herself. The rise in our standard of living throughout history has instead come from focusing more on specialized skills and delegating more life tasks to others who specialize in what they do best. You should be able not only to retire in style but to choose even more what you really want to do in life after your kids have left the nest.

The key to achieving your dreams is to understand the most fundamental trends driving our economy. Only then can you be clear enough to plan your life and to find and trust a competent advisor to put you on a systematic investment plan that you can feel good about. A plan you can stick with even when the markets are down 20% or more for a few months, as in late 1998. The greatest mistake is selling in such corrections and not buying more instead. But you can't have the conviction to do that even with the urging of a good financial advisor or mentor unless you understand the most fundamental of trends and know that the markets are heading higher.

It's not enough to trust long-term statistics that prove that stocks and equities provide superior returns over time. What if you had bought a blue chip stock portfolio in 1929? You would have suffered up to 90% losses into 1932 and had to wait until 1953 to break even. If you'd had to retire on that portfolio in the 1930s and 1940s, you would have been in deep trouble. The same would have occurred to a slightly lesser degree after 1968. Such a blue chip portfolio would have fallen 70% (adjusted for inflation) into 1982, and you would have had to wait until 1993 to break even.

The purpose of this book is to take a very different look at economic trends that I will summarize from my earlier books, *The Great Boom Ahead* and *The Roaring 2000s*. You can see all of the important trends that will affect your investments for decades to come. Just because economists don't understand our economy doesn't mean that you can't. Our economy is driven by the predictable habits of people like you. Hence, you will be able to understand how to prosper in good times (the next decade) and bad times (the decade to follow). But what I will do in this book is look at the nitty-gritty details, from the predictable changes in your cost of living to the specific sectors you need to be investing in to the intricate subtleties of tax and estate planning. And perhaps most important, how to choose the right financial advisor for you, someone who represents you, not a salesperson for investment products.

But let me start by giving a new, more summary view of the very simple generation-based trends that drive all the key long-term trends in our economy and investments.

The Generation Wave

The most important forecasting tool for our economy and the stock market in my past books is the spending wave shown in Chart 1-1. The peak of spending of the average family today in the United States (and in most developed countries) is age 46.5. This

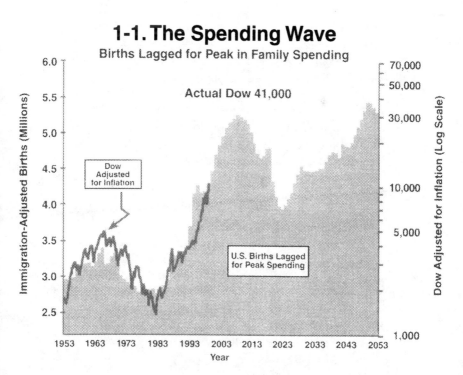

1-1. The Spending Wave
Births Lagged for Peak in Family Spending

Actual Dow 41,000

Dow Adjusted for Inflation

U.S. Births Lagged for Peak Spending

comes from reliable surveys of consumer spending taken every year by
the U.S. Bureau of Labor. I simply lag forward the birth index, adjusted for immigration, for this peak in spending, 46.5 years later. This
simple indicator will tell you when our economy and stock markets
will boom and when they will bust almost five decades in advance.
Refer to *The Roaring 2000s* for a more detailed explanation.

The critical insight is this: The massive baby boom generation
will drive spending and productivity trends higher into late 2008 to
mid-2009. Therefore, this unprecedented economic and stock market
boom will continue for the next decade. Then there will be an economic downturn that will change your life and your investments. You
have to plan for the boom and the bust today! And obviously your kids'
jobs and education prospects will be affected by this cycle.

And where do I see the stock market headed? Likely to around
40,000 on the Dow by 2008.

That may sound outrageous, but it's not. That is simply the same
16% average annual rate of increase on the Dow and S&P 500 since
this boom began in late 1982. Chart 1-2 shows the Dow channel of
growth on a ratio graph, or a constant rate of growth, instead of a normal numerical graph. It projects a peak of around 41,000 by late 2008,
even higher than my 35,000 forecast in *The Roaring 2000s*. If the
boom were to peak a year earlier, the top of the channel would be at
35,000. And it is likely that this top channel trend line would be ex-
ceeded briefly at the top of this bull market.

Note that the market has been transitioning from the lower
end of this channel since 1994 and has yet to hit the upper end
and achieve overvaluation to the same extent as in late 1987. That
also occurred in the last 26-year bull market from 1942 to 1968, when
valuations shifted to higher ranges from the mid-'50s into the
early '60s. That is why the gains in the stock markets have been so
extraordinary since 1995, averaging closer to 30% per year. By late
1999 to mid-2000 this valuation boom is likely to see its zenith, and
then we will have to settle for average annual gains more in the 14%
to 18% range into 2007–8. Gains of that magnitude will still double
your wealth every 4½ years! I will show in Chapter 2 how you can con-
struct a portfolio that can be positioned for potential gains in the 20%

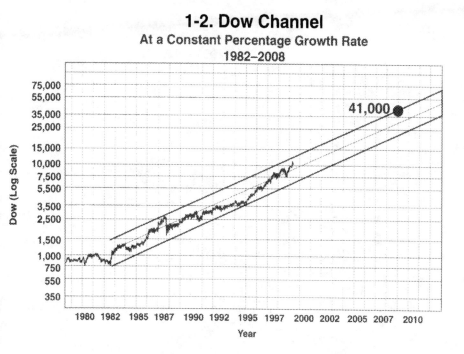

1-2. Dow Channel
At a Constant Percentage Growth Rate
1982–2008

to 24% range without taking significantly more risk than in an S&P 500 index fund. The Dow could hit the top of this channel between late summer or early fall. We could then see a sharp correction sometime between August and the end of the year that would represent a great buying opportunity.

There are two reasons I have shifted to this slightly more bullish channel since 1998. The first is the strength of the rebound from the late 1998 correction, which shifted the average growth rates even higher. But the most important reason is that this projection of 41,000 in 2008 also coincides very closely with a longer-term channel extending back to 1901 in Chart 1-3 (page 28). This channel projects a Dow of over 250,000 by 2040-plus, when the next generation's spending boom will be in strong force. But we could also see the Dow first go as low as 10,000 to 15,000 during the down phase of the generation cycle into 2020 to 2023.

1-3. Long-Term Dow Channel
At a Constant Percentage Growth Rate
1901–2050

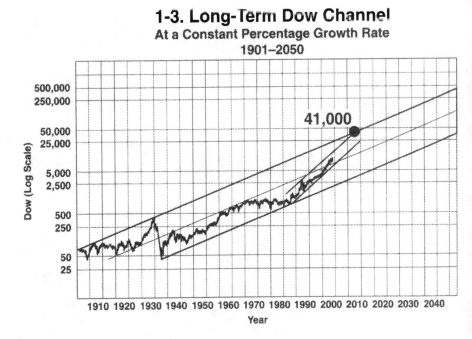

Generation Cycles Drive All Key Trends in Our Economy

Here's the summary insight. Every major trend in our economy—from earning and spending to saving and borrowing to inflation and innovation to productivity and business revolutions to our cradle-to-grave spending habits in every product and service industry—is driven by the predictable aging of new generations of consumers and workers. New generations come in waves about every 40 years, as we can see in Chart 1-4. These generation trends have been documented in great detail (before annual birth statistics were available) in two great books by William Strauss and Neil Howe: *Generations* (1989) and *The Fourth Turning* (1997). But for now, simply note the size of the baby boom generation when adjusted for the births of all legal immigrants compared to the Bob Hope generation wave before it. Everything that baby boomers do exaggerates every trend in our economy

1-4. Immigration-Adjusted Birth Index

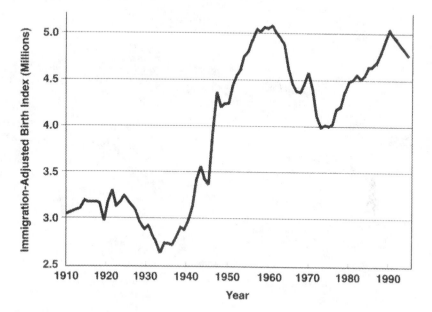

predictably. This is why you can see all the key economic trends decades in advance and plan your life and investments around them.

Let me summarize my full array of principles from *The Roaring 2000s* in two simpler charts. The first one, Chart 1-5 (page 30), summarizes the cycle of key events and expenditures in the life of the average consumer, which drives our economy as new generations move through these predictable cycles in peak numbers. As kids we need predictable things, from diapers to baby food. We enter kindergarten and elementary school and then junior high and high school. But let's start here with college. We have to build new colleges and universities as more people turn age 18.

Only after people enter the workforce, typically after high school or college, do these new generations become productive workers and consumers who earn and spend more money and drive economic

1-5. Key Consumer Expenditures/Investments

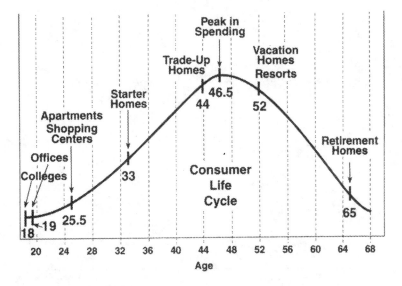

boom periods. They move into apartments as they get their first jobs, and demand for apartments peaks when they get married around age 25½ to 26 today. They suddenly need stores and shopping malls as they get married and form households. Shopping center development peaked in 1986, 25 years after the peak of the baby boom birth cycle in 1961. They have kids in their late twenties (age 27½ to 28, on average) and then buy starter homes into around age 33 and go into debt at the highest levels relative to their incomes by age 34 furnishing those homes. That's what caused the unprecedented rise in home prices into the late 1980s and the highest debt levels in history just after. The pressures of buying a house and raising kids cause most people to be very price sensitive and to favor discount stores and products (like Wal-Mart in the 1980s and early 1990s for baby boomers).

Then many trade up to better homes by age 44 and fully furnish them by age 46½ to 47, just when the kids leave the nest. Now they don't need a bigger house, more furnishings, more food in the refrigerator, and more clothes, and the average family spends less after age 47.

But empty-nest couples then spend more than ever on vacation homes, travel, and leisure into around age 52. Then, of course, we retire around age 65, driving up the cost of retirement homes, and spend the most on health care into our seventies and eighties. In *The Great Boom Ahead* and *The Roaring 2000s*, I described many more everyday things, from potato chips and food cycles to veterinary services to motorcycles and cars, and the entire cycle in real estate and housing purchases.

You can see how such predictable cycles in generation spending patterns drive our economy, from the most micro industries to the macro economy. That is the fundamental trend that drives our economy and investment trends: simply new generation waves of consumers and workers. Chart 1-4 (page 29) shows the massive size of the baby boom generation versus the Bob Hope generation, which was only magnified by a large immigration wave from 1978 into 1991. I have calculated legal immigrants into the birth index by adjusting for their age of entrance. This means I am still excluding illegal immigrants, who are substantial in numbers. The baby boom generation is roughly five times the size of the last generation birth wave! It is this massive generation that has and is exaggerating all economic trends, from school expansion in the '60s and '70s to the starter home boom and debt explosion of the '70s and '80s to the economic boom from 1982 into 2008. And now comes a savings and investment boom from the mid-'90s on. The baby boom's massive savings, along with their peak spending and productivity, will continue to elevate the stock market to unprecedented heights in the next decade.

The point: As a baby boomer or other investor, your best strategy is to bet on the predictable spending and saving trends of this massive generation, which will combine to drive the stock market up until 2007 or 2008. The sectors of the economy that will benefit the most will be technology, financial services, health care, and travel and leisure, which will boom as baby boomers enter their forties and fifties. An even greater baby boom in emerging third world countries will drive an international boom that will be even greater after the emerging-countries bust in 1997 and 1998. Japan is the only major developed country that will continue to suffer from a baby bust after World War II.

1-6. Key Economic Trends

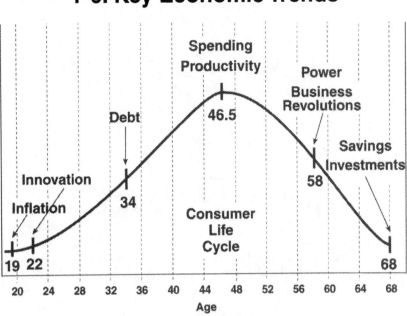

Chart 1-6 summarizes the key trends that drive our economy and investments that are caused by the generation cycle. Workforce entry averages around age 19 and is moving forward as more people go to college. Up until this point, young people represent a growing expense by parents and government to raise and educate them. When they enter the workforce, corporations have to train them and provide huge investments in office and work space, not to count the investments by governments and businesses in new technologies, infrastructures, and new companies' innovations that these new generations create. This is what causes inflation. Just ask yourself this commonsense question, true or false. Are young people expensive? Highly educated young people dominate innovations technologically and socially as they graduate from college around age 22. That's what drives innovation cycles in our economy.

Note that the highest rates of inflation in our country's history peaked in 1980, exactly 19 years after the peak of baby boom births.

And innovation or venture capital returns peaked in 1983, 22 years after the birth peak. As the generation cycle emerges, think of the first 19 to 22 years as high expense, high investment, and high innovation, and conversely low earnings, low productivity, and low spending. That is the first phase. The next phase brings the great economic boom periods. Rising earnings, spending, and productivity. The new technologies the generation innovated while young and the investments in infrastructures and training for them start to pay off. Here we see a booming economy for about 26 to 27 years (ages 19 to 46½ to 47½) with falling or low inflation rates.

Midpoint into their earning and spending years, we see a peak in debt ratios just after buying the first house and furnishing it around age 34. That is why we saw unprecedented debt ratios into the late 1980s and mid-1990s. Now debt levels are leveling off and even falling. Then we see the real economic revolutions as the new generation moves into its power years, from its forties to its sixties, peaking around age 58. That is when they control most companies and institutions, including governments. That is when they also have increasing savings and investment capital to create real change (savings accounts grow dramatically from the late thirties to around age 67 to 68). That is when you see the real work and management revolutions that fully leverage the technological and social innovations that began when the generation was young and innovative. That is when new technologies and products become mass affordable. That is when management and work revolutions occur that change how we work and live and advance our standard of living the most.

Economic and Technology Revolutions Every 80 Years

There is another important dimension that I covered in my past books. Every other generation (as documented by Strauss and Howe's research) is individualistic and change oriented. Every other generation we get the radical new technologies and social trends that create a whole new economy. The generations that follow are more conformist, civic-minded, and collective oriented, like the Bob Hope generation. The Henry Ford generation brought us electric motors, telephones, cars, movies, planes, and much more when they were young and innovative, from the mid-1870s into the early 1900s. The next generation's innovations were more incremental. They extended the new industries further into mass-market affordability and saturation.

The Bob Hope generation's innovations included power steering and brakes, automatic transmissions, and superhighways for cars and, of course, the jet engine for planes. The economy peaks in saturation with the spending cycle of the conformist generation, as occurred into the late '60s and early '70s with the Bob Hope generation boom. Then the next entrepreneurial generation comes along and creates the next innovations that drive a new economy, as the baby boomers did from the late '50s into the early '80s. Their spending then drives these new technologies, industries, and products into the economy, and their power years bring in radical new approaches to work and management, such as the assembly line revolution from 1914 to 1945 and the network revolution from 1994 into 2025 that is just now emerging with the explosive growth of the Internet.

So about every 80 years or every two generations, we see an economic revolution that starts when the entrepreneurial generation is young. These revolutions get ushered into the mainstream of our economy when the entrepreneurial generation moves into its peak spending and productivity years and the beginning of its real power years. This occurred for the last entrepreneurial generation, the Henry Ford generation, in the Roaring '20s. The massive baby boom will move into this powerful spending and productivity period of work and management change in the Roaring 2000s, the next decade, from around 2002 to 2008 or 2009. There are many predictable changes that will occur that you can profit from in your investments.

I summarize the network revolution in management that will make the re-engineering revolution look like child's play, or let's say the appetizer instead of the main course, in Part 3 of *The Roaring 2000s*. Chart 1-7 shows how we are moving on an 80-year cycle from an economy that made standardized products and services increasingly mass affordable to one that will make customized products and services mass affordable. Finally, we as consumers will get the type of personalized service that companies have only been promising in the past decades. We are about to enter a new era of prosperity. Actually, it already began in the mid-1990s.

Here's a summary chart of the economic and investment cycles

1-7. The New Customized Economy

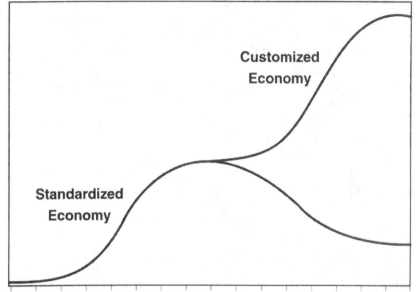

that are generated predictably over each 80-year economic revolution and with each 40-year generation cycle within. But first remember that we are in the midst of a more massive 500-year cycle. Every 500 years or so, the population of the world explodes, quadrupling or more in a century. These massive generation waves of new people drive even larger innovation cycles, such as those initiated by the printing press and the discovery of America and the scientific revolution to follow from the 1500s forward. Ever since the printing press, the last information revolution, we have been in a rising cycle of mass production. Now with the recent explosion in world population and the computer revolution, we are entering the beginning of an 80-year cycle of mass customization, a cycle that will continue over the next 500 years or so. This represents a greater revolution than we can imagine. We haven't seen the real information revolution yet. It is just emerging, as the printing press revolution did in the late 1400s and early 1500s, and as the car, phone, and electric motor revolution did in the Roaring '20s.

Over this two-generation cycle in which new economies emerge, there is a recurring four-stage cycle, as shown in Chart 1-8. Each stage favors certain asset categories of investments and disfavors others. Perhaps this is the most critical insight of this book.

> There are four distinct stages and six investment phases in the economic cycle that require very different long-term investment strategies. If you understand this cycle, you can prosper in good times and bad times.

It is great news that the current bull market will continue until around 2008. But the reality is that we will face a deflationary downturn after 2009 that will last until around 2022 to 2023. Baby boomers will be moving into their most important preretirement years of investment accumulation when most stock markets will be down! That

1-8. Economic Cycle and Investment Strategies

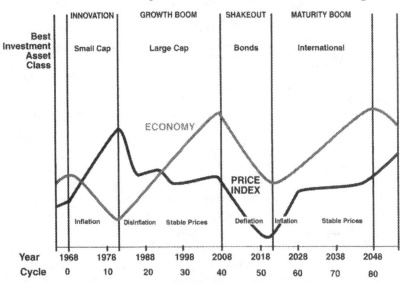

means your retirement could be more threatened by that downturn than by your failure to save in the past or the bankruptcy of Social Security. And your career and earnings capacity may be in jeopardy after 2009 as well. Let's review this 80-year economic cycle and summarize each stage, emphasizing the two phases ahead.

STAGE 1: *Inflation and Innovation*

The first stage starts as the young, new, individualistic generation is entering the workforce during a long-term recession period resulting from the downward spending wave of the previous, conformist generation. The last example would have been late 1968 into late 1982. The Bob Hope generation had peaked in its spending, causing a wave of recessions in 1970, 1974–75, 1980, and 1982. Inflation rose to the highest sustained levels in history. We saw the monumental microcomputer revolution emerge, from the first computer on a chip in 1971 by Intel to the first popular personal computer by Apple in 1977 to the start-up of Microsoft in 1983. Venture capital and start-up activity peaked between 1979 and 1983. In this period a new economy began to emerge, and that is always an inflationary process due to the huge investments it takes to retool for new infrastructures, new technologies, new companies, and the incorporation of a new generation into the workforce.

In the previous 80-year economic cycle, involving the emergence of cars, electrical appliances, and phones, the inflationary phase occurred from around 1898 into 1916. Since immigration created the greatest numbers of the Henry Ford generation, this cycle was abbreviated. Immigrants come into this country around age 30, on average. They spur innovation and infrastructure expansion on a shorter fuse (about a two-year lag) and are about 11 years older than the average native-born worker when they enter the workforce. Immigration surged at unprecedented rates beginning in 1898 and peaked in 1914 with the advent of World War I. Inflation rates continued to rise past the normal 1916 peak (based on a two-year lag on labor force growth) into 1920 because of the huge costs of the war effort. Then inflation fell dramatically from 1920 into 1921 because of the winding down of the war effort, creating a recession before the Roaring '20s were ushered in. We saw a peak in start-up activity of today's Fortune 500 and mass-market brand names between 1900 and 1907, a little less than 80 years from the peak in start-up activity between 1979 to 1983 in the recent cycle.

The best investments in Stage 1 are:
- Real estate, especially commercial
- Small company stocks
- Select international regions for stocks
- T-bills and CDs
- Gold

Real estate booms because a new generation is starting to enter the real estate cycle. This starts with new offices and industrial space (which peak with workforce entry around age 19), then apartments and multifamily rentals (which peak around age 26 with marriage), and then starter homes (which peak around age 33). Obviously, in the earlier part of this cycle, commercial real estate is the best investment. In the latter part apartments do better and starter homes begin to emerge with significant force. But real estate across the board also booms because of inflation. Real estate is a leveraged hedge (due to mortgages) against inflation for investors. So this is the best overall investment in what can seem to be very turbulent times of inflation and innovation.

Small company stocks also do very well even when the overall stock market is declining because of worsening recession and inflation. Why small company stocks? Because a new generation is innovating new technologies, products, and social trends. Small companies are more nimble at exploiting such new niche markets, while large companies are slow to change and adapt. What's more, the large companies are losing their loyal customers from the last generation, who are becoming savers, not spenders. In fact, this brings us to another critical insight:

Small companies outperform large companies dramatically in off periods of recession and innovation. Large companies outperform to a smaller degree in sustained boom periods in which niche markets move mainstream.

1-9. Small Caps Outperform in Inflationary Times

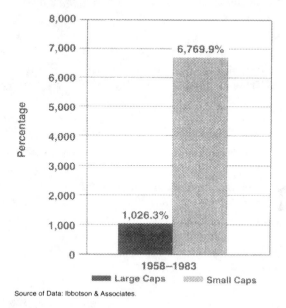

Source of Data: Ibbotson & Associates.

Many financial experts tell us to diversify our portfolios between large and small company stocks. The truth is they do well at very different times, and this is a disastrous way to diversify our portfolios. Therefore, we should emphasize small company stocks in the off periods and large company stocks increasingly in the boom periods. Chart 1-9 proves this point conclusively. The innovation phase of the baby boom generation was from 1958 into 1983 on a 22-year lag to its birth cycle. Small cap stocks outperformed large caps more than 6 to 1 on a cumulative basis! This period culminated in the inflation-recession stage from 1968 to 1982. However, the best time to have bought small cap stocks was after the extreme 1974 crash, as they got hammered even more than large cap stocks in that short period. Most of the outperformance from 1958 to 1983, 4 to 1 in cumulative returns, occurred from 1974 to 1983. An important rule of thumb is to buy small company stocks as we enter a long-term down period in the economy and stock market **only** after a large crash in the stock market of at least 50% from the top, preferably 70% (using stock indexes adjusted for inflation). I will show in the section on the deflationary stage that small caps also outperform similarly.

The 1970s also saw the boom really get started in Japan while many third world countries benefited from rising resource prices. Selective investment internationally can reward the investor in such a cycle. Japan has a very different generation and birth cycle from those of most other developed countries and was booming in the 1970s while the United States and Europe were busting. I will show Japan's birth and economic cycles in Chapter 3. Although there was money to be made in emerging country stocks, the volatility, especially in 1974, was too much for most investors. That's why I stress "selective" when talking about international investments. Japan represented a solid developed country with strong growth and low inflation due to its counter-cyclical generation trends. That would have been another great place to invest in the 1970s.

The investments to avoid are obviously large cap stocks, but also intermediate and long-term bonds. Rising inflation causes bonds with longer-term maturities to depreciate as new bonds are issued with higher, more attractive rates as inflation rises. Very short-term debt instruments like T-bills and CDs allow investors to constantly trade up to higher short-term rates. This is where conservative investors who need income should concentrate. Gold as a hedge against inflation also does well in such a period, although that may not occur as much in future inflationary stages as gold loses its function as a monetary metal in the information age.

STAGE 2: *The Growth Boom*

As the individualistic generation enters its spending wave, the economy starts to boom again, and inflation starts to fall as the new generation and its new technologies drive increased productivity. The spending wave in Chart 1-1 (page 25) shows how the massive baby boom started our present boom in late 1982. The new generation increasingly buys the new products and technologies as their spending power grows. That causes them to emerge from niche, luxury markets increasingly into the mainstream, especially as the productivity from new technologies makes them more affordable. This creates a race for leadership to see which companies will dominate these new mass markets, from computers to specialty coffees. Hence, large company stocks increasingly outperform small company stocks, as we can see in Chart 1-10. But large company stocks don't outperform by nearly as wide a margin as small caps do in the off periods, more like 2 to 1 in cumulative returns since 1984. That gap could widen in the coming decade.

Large company stocks seemed to trounce small company stocks in the growth boom of the Roaring '20s. There are data only for the last four years, from 1926 through 1929, from Ibbotson and Associates, but in that period large cap stocks averaged 19.8%, compared to a

1-10. Large Caps Outperform in Growth Booms

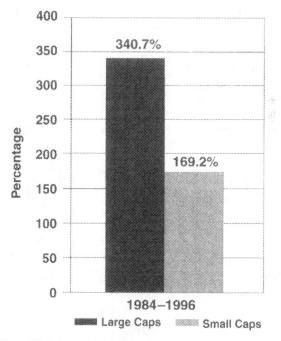

Source of Data: Ibbotson & Associates.

4.5% loss for small caps. But as the smaller echo baby boom generation enters its innovation phase from 1998 on, small caps will do better
than in the past.

This growth boom period of about 26 to 27 years actually splits
into two phases, the first with falling inflation, the second with relatively flat inflation. That means two different investment portfolio
strategies.

PHASE 1: Falling Inflation Rates

Inflation falls dramatically during this phase, creating the best performance you will see from long-term bonds and fixed-income securities.
From 1981 into 1998 inflation rates fell from about 14% to near zero.
The average return from 30-year U.S. Treasury bonds was 13.9%. That
wasn't quite as good as the S&P 500, but given that you were guaranteed to get your interest and principal, this was a great time for investors who needed fixed income and were averse to taking risk. And
your bonds appreciated in value from falling inflation and interest
rates when you sold them.

During this phase the real estate cycle remains strong in starter
homes, the greatest expenditure phase in the real estate cycle. Therefore, residential home prices boom the most in this period, especially
in the earlier phase, as they did from late 1982 into early 1990 in this
boom cycle. The new generation buys more starter homes into age 33,
which creates a plateau in starter home buying, as occurred from 1990
into 1994 on a 33-year lag of the peak baby boom birth rates from 1957
to 1961. Then starter home demand grows slower than the economy.
Commercial real estate falls off in demand on about a 19-year lag as
workforce entry peaks just before the boom starts. Phase 1 of the
growth boom occurred from late 1982 into early 1998 in the baby
boom cycle.

The best investments in Phase 1 of the growth boom are:
- Residential real estate
- Large cap stocks
- Long-term bonds

PHASE 2: Low, Flat Inflation Rates

This is the phase we have entered since 1998. As new technologies create very strong productivity and as the new generation ages into its most productive years (in the midforties), inflation settles into a low or near-zero range. This occurred in the Roaring '20s as well. This means that bonds offer very low yields and little or no appreciation potential from falling inflation rates. Bonds are the worst investment in this phase. Large cap stocks continue to outperform as the race for leadership comes to a head in the latter phases of the boom. But small cap stocks may fare a bit better after 1998, when the innovation wave of the echo baby boom kicks in. Trade-up homes and increasingly vacation home and resort real estate boom even more strongly in the real estate sectors. Lagging international regions tend to be forced to catch up to the business practices of the leading nations (like the United States in this economic revolution). Therefore, international equities do well in nations that have strong spending waves from aging new generations.

The best investments for Phase 2 of the growth boom are:

- Large company stocks
- International stocks
- Resort and high-end residential real estate

STAGE 3: *Deflationary Shakeout*

The next stage is the worst for most investors and workers but the best for the most financially savvy. It is the depression era, in which we see falling prices or deflation and very high unemployment rates. This period is not an innovative period of bringing in fresh new technologies or industries. It is a time when the economy shakes out the remaining companies that didn't win the race for leadership. This means divesting productive facilities and laying off workers. The few remaining leaders in each industry absorb the market share and the most productive facilities and workers from the failing companies. This stage of the last economic cycle came between 1930 and 1942. Stocks were generally down dramatically from late 1929 into 1932. Prices fell equally dramatically from 1930 into 1933. Stocks lost 90% of their value, and real estate prices plummeted. Stocks were still down 70% in 1942 when the next bull market started. Of course, such deflationary times were good for long-term bonds. There was a flight to quality from equities, and falling prices resulted in falling bond yields. From late 1929 into 1942, yields on the 30-year U.S. Treasury bond fell from about 3.5% to 2%. That means bonds appreciated in value as interest rates fell. More important, principal and interest were guaranteed in abysmal times and unstable conditions. And money bought more because of falling prices of everything from food to housing. Investors had to adjust for deflation in those times. From 1930 to 1942, total returns on long-term government bonds averaged 3.5%; and on corporate bonds, 6.19%. Such returns of 3.5% to 6.1% were worth more like 6% to 9% in real purchasing power value. Not as good as the stock yields in the boom periods, but very good compared to other investments that were mostly falling. In a deflationary period, bonds generally bring the best risk/return ratios.

And it shouldn't surprise you too much at this point to learn that small company stocks did very well, but again only after the crash. Chart 1-11 shows from 1932 to 1946 that small company stocks outperformed by a margin of about 6 to 1 on cumulative returns in just a 14-year period. That is astounding!

The same logic applies as in inflationary periods. A new generation is entering the economy, innovating and buying new technologies and products. The smaller companies are more adept at attacking these new markets. However, there is a difference in the nature of innovation. These are incremental innovations that extend the growth industries that emerged in the growth stage. But it still takes smaller companies to give birth to these new innovations at first.

There is another valuable trend to understand in this very turbulent period. In *The Roaring 2000s*, in Chapter 10, I show how new technology revolutions eventually cause a shift in population to new areas where the quality of life is higher and the cost of living is lower. The massive shift from the cities to the suburbs accelerated from the 1930s into the 1960s because of the mass adoption of cars, phones, and home electrification. The mass adoption of the Internet (which I also cover in Part 2 of *The Roaring 2000s*) between 1994 and 2008 will

1-11. Small Caps Outperform in Deflationary Downturns

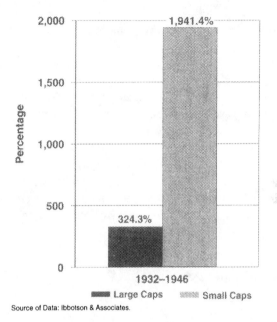

Source of Data: Ibbotson & Associates.

also cause a massive shift to exurban areas outside the suburbs of large cities and to attractive small resort towns. Therefore, the new growth areas in real estate are great investments in depression periods but, like small cap stocks, best after the crash in stocks and real estate values.

The best investments in Stage 3 are:

- Long-term government and very high quality corporate bonds
- Small cap stocks (only after the crash)
- Exurban real estate and commercial real estate (especially after the crash)

STAGE 4: *The Maturity Boom*

When the next, or conformist, generation enters its spending cycle, we see a boom wherein the industries of the last revolution move fully into mainstream market saturation. In the last 80-year cycle, that would have been 1942 into 1968 for the Bob Hope generation. These booms favor large and small cap stocks, residential real estate, and international equities. Large cap stocks tend to do better in the first half of the boom, and small cap stocks start to outperform in the second half as the next individualistic generation starts to move into its innovative stage, creating the radical innovations for spawning the next economy and 80-year cycle. The next maturity boom will begin around 2023 with the millennial generation and last until about 2050. But that is too far off to concentrate on for now. Note that, as in the growth booms, there are two phases that slightly favor different investments.

The best investments in Stage 4 are:
- Large cap stocks (first and second phase)
- Small cap stocks (second phase)
- Residential real estate (first phase)
- Commercial real estate (second phase)
- International stocks (second phase)

There tends to be a slight inflationary bias in this phase that does not favor long-term bonds. And again, in the second half of the boom, international stocks tend to follow the practices of leading nations like the United States and perform well.

Portfolio Strategies for the Next Decade

Given that we are entering the second phase of the growth boom, you as an investor should be focusing on large cap equities, international equities, and exurban, resort, and high-end residential real estate. The next generation will also cause rising values in rental and multifamily housing. Small cap stocks greatly underperformed from

1995 into 1998 and got trounced in the correction of 1998. Therefore, they may outperform a bit into 2000 or so. But large caps should rule in the next decade of the Roaring 2000s. In Chapter 2, I will look at how to create a portfolio of mutual funds or large cap stocks to beat the S&P 500 with minimal risks by being in the best sectors that will be leveraged by baby boomers.

In Part 2, I will take a look at the most exciting arena of this portfolio strategy for the coming decade. Note that while large cap stocks in the United States have achieved high valuations, many international markets have experienced the worst beating since the mid-1970s. There is great value in understanding which countries have the potential to outperform in the coming decade and which ones don't. Japan is a country that will clearly underperform, whereas its neighbors, like Hong Kong, South Korea, Singapore, and Taiwan, will very likely outperform in the coming decade. A look at the simple age demographics and technological trends throughout the world will make us very savvy investors in the coming decade and beyond. In Chapter 3, I will look at the demographic and technological prospects for the more-developed countries around the world, using the very simple indicators I have used for the United States.

But remember that the greatest population increases in the last century occurred in emerging countries. In Chapter 4, I will look at the prospects for growth in the massive populations of the emerging third world nations. The massive growth trends around the world in the coming decade will only serve to further leverage the larger companies that can expand efficiently overseas with proven brand names here. This is another reason to be invested in the largest company leaders in old and new industries over the coming decade, as opposed to small company stocks, except in exciting new areas like biotech and e-commerce.

In Part 3, I will look at the lifestyle dimensions of planning your life, from where you can live to what the cost of living will likely be well into the future. And finally, in Part 4, I will look at how to find a competent financial advisor who will represent you and how to leverage your wealth with simple tax strategies.

Let's first look at how to create the ultimate portfolio for the Roaring 2000s!

CHAPTER 2
The Ultimate Portfolio Strategy for the Roaring 2000s

THE MOST POWERFUL INNOVATION in investing that has emerged in this information revolution has been the principle of asset allocation. If mutual funds and other packaged investment products like index funds and unit investment trusts represent the PCs of the investment revolution, then asset allocation represents the basic operating system software, like Windows. To explain the principle of asset allocation simply, you can increase the returns of your investment portfolio and/or reduce the risk if you scientifically diversify among several different classes of investments that move up and down in dissimilar or "noncorrelating" patterns. For example, bonds and stocks tend to move up and down for different reasons at different times. A downturn in the economy can be bad for the earnings of stocks but cause declining inflation rates, which are good for bonds, and vice versa for an upturn. It is often true that large and small company stocks thrive at different times in the economic cycle. And of course, different countries can boom or bust on very different cycles.

The academic and industry research that has spawned this powerful principle has documented back to 1926 (where adequate data were available) that the best risk versus return ratios for investors resulted from combining the four most basic categories with low correlation rates. The four categories are large company stocks, small company stocks, international stocks, and fixed income (bonds and interest-bearing securities). The breakthrough research that spawned these insights started with Harry Markowitz in the 1950s and has been extended by many, most notably Roger Ibbotson, in recent decades. Although this is perhaps the greatest theory to emerge in investing, it has a very serious flaw.

The One Great Flaw in Modern Investment Theory

As many financial advisors I work with will tell you, this is a great principle, but it more often than not does not work in practice. The strategy does often reduce risk or volatility, but it tends most consistently to reduce returns versus the S&P 500, especially over the past two decades. What I am going to show here is that there is nothing wrong with the theory; it is simply how the asset classes are applied to real-life portfolios that is the problem. Remember that the research to document the risks and returns benefits from diversifying portfolios in the classes above has been based on average returns over 70 years of data. How many of us have a 70-year time horizon for investing?

Most people don't start saving and investing seriously until they are in their late thirties, save the most from their late forties into their mid-fifties, and accumulate their greatest net worth around age 67 to 68. That means that, on average, our typical time horizon is more like 15 to 30 years. Younger investors obviously have longer time horizons, and people nearing retirement have much shorter ones. But even within these time horizons we have different needs for income, from college to retirement, that may shorten our time horizons. And perhaps most important, our human tendencies and natural emotional reactions to economic changes can often make our time horizons much shorter. Therefore, the first flaw is that the research that produced this theory doesn't match our real-life investment horizons.

The bigger error comes from the fact that our economy goes through very different medium- to long-term cycles within the two-generation or 80-year cycle that I outlined in Chapter 1. Since 1926, when the data for most asset allocation research started, there have been dramatic changes in our economy and investing environment:

- The Roaring '20s, an extreme boom period with low, flat inflation rates and very high productivity rates in business from the assembly-line revolution
- The terrible '30s, or Great Depression, the worst downturn in history, with unemployment rates as high as 25% and extreme deflation in prices
- The 1940s, including World War II, when we saw growth again, but rising inflation
- The 1950s and 1960s, a booming economy with low inflation rates
- The 1970s, a recession period with dramatically rising inflation rates, the highest in modern history
- The 1980s, a boom period with dramatically falling inflation rates
- The 1990s, the boom continues with modestly declining inflation rates and surging productivity from the information revolution
- And next, the Roaring 2000s, as I am forecasting, a period like the Roaring '20s but stronger, with flat inflation rates and very strong productivity and growth

Let me ask you a simple question. Do you think that the same investment strategy would have worked for each of these very different cycles over the last 70 to 80 years? In each change of cycle, the investments that were thriving suddenly became the dogs of the next cycle. And these cycles lasted a decade or more, not just a few years. For example, in the Roaring '20s it was large company stocks that did the best, while bonds and small company stocks languished. In the 1930s large company stocks did the worst, while bonds were king and small company stocks surged again after the crash. In the 1970s the best large cap stocks of the 1960s were massacred, but so were bonds by rising inflation rates. Small company stocks were the heroes, along with real estate and select international sectors like Japan and many emerging countries.

And now in the 1980s and 1990s, large company stocks are increasingly trouncing small company stocks and international stocks, while bonds have done well. Investors who have been following the traditional asset allocation model by diversifying into large company, small company, international, and bonds have been underperforming the S&P 500 index since 1983, albeit at slightly lower rates of volatility. As I forecast in Chapter 1, large company stocks should continue to lead in the coming decade, while international stocks should make a strong comeback. Small company stocks will continue to lag at a lesser rate, while bonds will represent the lowest returns by far because of low, flat inflation rates.

In Chapter 1, I outlined four very different economic stages over the 80-year economic cycle, with two phases within each boom period. This gives us six distinct investment environments over our average life span. Please take the time to review these cycles and the investment categories that are strong and weak in each phase. In each of these cycles lasting around 10 to 16 years each, it is typical for two out of the four asset classes used for asset allocation to underperform substantially, if not dramatically. Therefore, in practice, the traditional approach to asset allocation actually produces lower returns than you would receive if you systematically invested in the best two sectors. Obviously, we shouldn't have the same strategies over these very different cycles. And since the basic trends in economic growth, inflation, and innovation are fundamentally predictable in each phase of this cycle, we don't have to!

That summarizes the massive flaw in asset allocation theory. The theory averaged out the effects of all of these very different economic cycles over a time horizon that almost none of us would relate to in real life. It therefore produces very suboptimal returns for investors. Although it does tend to lower risk or volatility of returns, that reduction in risk is not commensurate with the reduction in returns. The 10- to 16-year economic cycles that emerge in our economy not only offer distinct opportunities for profiting from systematic investing strategies but also better fit a time horizon for planning that ordinary mortals can relate to, even if retirement is decades away.

Positioning Your Investments for the Roaring 2000s

Since late 1982 we have been in the growth boom stage of the 80-year cycle. This phase follows the inflationary innovation stage. Hence, we see declining inflation rates. But this stage is most characterized by the rising spending wave of an individualistic generation, which brings not only a booming economy but the rise of new industries into the mainstream and the highest productivity rates. As the innovative new industries of the previous stage move increasingly into the mainstream economy, larger companies dominate even those new industries. Therefore, large company stocks increasingly outperform, as I showed in Chart 1-10 on page 41. But remember that each boom stage splits into two phases.

The first phase of the growth boom sees declining inflation rates, but with more modest rises in productivity rates. This phase occurred from late 1982 into 1998, or 16 years, as is typical. In that first phase the two best investment categories are large company stocks and long-term bonds. The bonds do well because falling interest rates cause yields locked in at higher rates to become more valuable; hence, the price of those bonds appreciates. International and small company stocks underperformed predictably in that first phase.

But in the second phase you see low, flat inflation rates, which make bonds the worst investment category. Small company stocks continue to underperform, but the international sectors should thrive after the huge stock crash between 1997 and 1998. That crisis not only created attractive valuations on most foreign stocks but will force most world economies to move more toward the very free-market economic policies that have been pioneered in the United States and are being favored by the information revolution. The demographic trends in many parts of the world are even stronger than in the United States, as I will demonstrate in great detail in Part 2.

This second phase kicked in around late 1994 as earnings, especially of large company stocks, surged incredibly as the Internet started to move mainstream for the first time. As we move into the next decade, I expect the large company and international sectors to reward investors the most. So the question is, How do you diversify into several sectors to optimize your portfolio if you have only two sectors to choose from? Or worse, only one if you prefer to avoid the occasional chaos of the international sectors?

The answer comes from understanding another simple principle. The four broad asset classes used in traditional asset allocation theory are not the only investment sectors that move in different patterns and hence can be effective for diversification. There are many major sectors of our domestic economy and many sectors of the international economy that have different patterns of price movement, as well as different levels of risk, to meet the needs of different investors.

Within international sectors there is a vast difference in risks and returns among major regions like Europe, Asia, and Latin America. There are great differences between the more mature and stable developed countries and the younger, more politically volatile emerging countries. After all, the international crisis from late 1997 into 1998 was centered in emerging countries, not in developed ones. And even more conservative investors who don't want to risk their money on political trends overseas can invest in the very-low-risk large multinational companies in the United States that are growing largely overseas, with incredible diversification and proven product and management models that we can understand. They even manage the currency risks for investors.

Domestically, there are choices ranging from more conservative staple products like utilities and basic foods to high-growth technology stocks. There are many sectors to choose from to fit your risk profile that also diversify well with other sectors and all within the large company stock sector that my research strongly suggests will outperform in the coming decade.

A Sound Strategy for Beating the S&P 500

I have spent much time analyzing the returns and risk levels of the different sectors of our economy. In fact, that's largely where I focus my research on investments now, as I see that the key to strong returns in the coming decade is simply picking the best sectors. Everyone has been getting hip to the superior performance of large company stocks and the S&P 500, Dow, and Nasdaq 100 indexes that best capture them. But I am not recommending that you buy just an S&P 500 index fund for the next decade, although that would be a good strategy, especially if you had the discipline to stick with it (which most investors don't).

How do you beat the S&P 500? With the best sectors of the S&P 500! You can pick higher-return sectors that are benefiting from fundamental trends and combine them for effective diversification. Such a strategy allows you to actually achieve the original promises of asset allocation research in this real-life period of low inflation and large company dominance.

| You can raise your returns and/or lower your risks by combining various high-growth large company sectors that will be favored by predictable demographic and technological trends and also have shown the propensity to diversify each sector's risks.

Before I present what I see as the ultimate portfolio for a growth investor in the coming decade, let me summarize my approach to choosing these "power alley" investment sectors:

1. I preferred sectors that have been outperforming since 1990. I used 1990 to 1998 as my evaluation period for two reasons. First is that it largely represented similar trends to what I am projecting in the next decade: healthy economic growth, low inflation rates, and strong rises in productivity. Late 1994 into 1998 especially reflected this phase of the growth boom stage. I expect lower, more stable inflation rates and even higher rates of productivity over the next decade into 2008. But I also went back to 1990 in order to capture enough time data and to include four substantial corrections (late 1990, early 1994, late 1997, and mid- to late 1998) for gauging volatility and risk.

2. Most important, I wanted sectors that should be expected to continue to outperform in the coming decade based on projectable demographic and technological trends. It is always easy to select high-performing sectors from the past. Often those sectors will underperform in the future. That is one of the greatest investment mistakes, to assume that strong sectors will stay strong. I wanted sectors that you as an investor could reasonably expect to continue to remain strong for the next decade.

3. These preferred sectors also had to show evidence that they diversified well in a portfolio to balance the other high-performing sectors' risk and volatility. That means that they moved up and down in different patterns or showed clear evidence of what is called "low correlation" in investment standards.

4. And finally, these sectors had to be of significant size that investors could target them through specialty mutual funds, index funds, or small clusters of leading large company stocks.

The domestic sectors that best satisfied these criteria were technology, financial services, health care, large multinational companies (typified by the Dow stocks), and Asia (excluding Japan). Note that the large leading-brand multinational sector is an effective way to play the international growth trends that I favor for the coming decade, as I mentioned earlier.

Technology

That technology stocks will continue to outperform in the coming decade should be obvious. If the Internet and computers are moving mainstream on an accelerated S curve, much like cars in the Roaring '20s, then this sector should see its best years ahead, even after already outperforming in the past decade. The best returns for the risk I found were in the software sectors of technology. If you add the rapid rise of the Internet, then software, systems integration, and Internet stocks should be the leading sectors in high tech for the next decade.

Financial Services

Financial services not only is a high-value-added, knowledge-intensive industry that will benefit greatly from technological progress but is probably the strongest major sector for demographic trends in the coming decade. The massive baby boom will just be entering its saving and investment cycle en masse for the first time in the coming decade. The average household begins saving in their mid- to late thirties and continues into their late sixties, as I explained in depth in *The Roaring 2000s*. This means that the savings cycle follows the spending cycle (ages 19 to 47) by approximately 16 to 20 years! The baby boom spending cycle started in late 1982, and their investment cycle is just taking off and should accelerate more dramatically after the turn of the century, from 2002 on.

There are only 12 years in our life cycle in which we spend and save aggressively at the same time, and that is between the ages of 35 and 47. That is where the baby boom generation will be in the largest numbers in history from 1998 into 2008–9. That will be not only a great time for the economy but a golden era for financial services, especially on the investment side. I expect financial services to be the best domestic sector outside technology. It could even rival the technology sector as a whole in the coming decade. Investment management and brokerage stocks should do the best. Basic banking and lending will grow slower, as will insurance. But there will be many opportunities from banks and insurance companies that successfully enter or merge into the investment and tax/estate-planning side of the business.

Health Care

Health care is the only major sector of our economy that grows over our entire lifetime. Baby boomers have already been causing this sector to outperform, and the trend will continue for a long time, not just for the next decade. Like financial services, this sector is also knowledge and information intensive and should benefit from the information revolution to a greater degree than most industries. Perhaps most important, we are consistently spending a higher percentage of our GDP on health care.

Why? Because there are more options than ever for extending our life span and improving our quality of life. And most of us value that increasingly over other categories of spending. I think that trend will continue, don't you? And the biotech revolution is just starting to emerge into practical health applications. Although this sector has not and is not likely to show returns quite as high as those in technology and financial services, it is steadier in its growth and less volatile, making it a great diversifier in your portfolio. The best sectors should be pharmaceuticals/drugs, biotech, and outpatient care/home services. Since biotech is still in its early stages, small company stocks are likely to outperform large company stocks at first.

Large Multinational Companies

The Dow has just slightly outperformed the S&P 500 in the last decade because it is concentrated even more in the large company and international trends. Although exhibiting slightly lower returns than the above sectors since 1990, this sector had the best risk versus return ratios. These companies tend to dominate rapidly growing markets for products and services that are already mature in the United

States and/or Europe and Japan. These companies tend to be highly diversified around the world and even manage much of the currency risks for investors. Hence, they have high margins and high growth rates with low volatility rates, as Warren Buffet calculated a long time ago. Like health care, this sector brings not only the benefits of international growth and diversification but lower risk and volatility to a domestic portfolio.

Asia and Other International Sectors

The other way to invest in international trends is to select country or regional funds. Obviously, developed country funds that focus on regions like Europe are less risky than funds that focus on newly industrializing countries like Hong Kong or South Korea, which in turn are less risky than funds that focus on emerging countries like Indonesia, Brazil, or South Africa. Hence, there exists a wide range of options for investors with different returns and tolerances for risks. Since international markets have exhibited substantially higher risks and volatility than the Dow and S&P 500, my preferred strategy is to invest in those sectors when they take major corrections. By doing this, you not only buy at better value but can minimize the downside risk of these more volatile markets.

The best long-term returns and the best diversification impact from 1990 to 1998 came in Asia, excluding Japan. And Asia also took the greatest beating between late 1997 and late 1998, creating incredible value for long-term investing. With the strongest demographic trends and rates of urban migration, I expect Asia to continue to be the strongest international sector in the coming decade. Asia will represent one of the few major regions of relative strength in the years following 2009.

The Ultimate Growth Portfolio for the Roaring 2000s

Let me now present what I see as the optimal strong growth portfolio for the coming decade, plus many alternatives to follow for making such a portfolio more aggressive or more conservative. By combining the sectors presented above in the optimum combinations,

2-1. Aggressive Growth Portfolio
January 1990 through March 1999

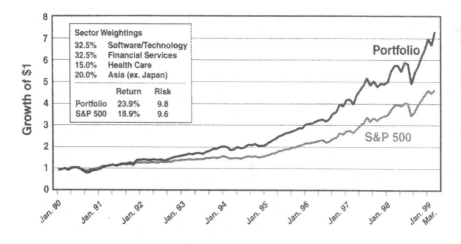

you would have beat the S&P 500 from 1990 to 1998 by as much as 5 percentage points annually on average, with a risk or volatility level just slightly higher. You can see the advantage in performance of this growth portfolio versus the S&P 500 over the nine years from January 1, 1990, through March 31, 1999, in Chart 2-1. The difference is that a $10,000 investment would have grown to $74,000 versus $47,000. That's a 57% better cumulative return and an over sevenfold increase in just nine years.

This portfolio averaged 23.9% average annual returns, versus the S&P 500 average of 18.9%. But the astounding statistic here is that the volatility or risk level measured by what analysts call the standard deviation was only 9.8, just slightly higher than the S&P 500 at 9.6. Now, any good financial advisor will tell you that if you can raise your returns by 5 percentage points per year, or 26%, with an increase in the volatility of 0.2, or just 2%, you will have achieved a near miracle in investing. Obviously, as an investor, you can't be assured that these same returns and volatility levels will continue in the future. But my research strongly suggests that these sectors will continue to perform strongly in the coming eight to ten years. And experts have found that the risk or volatility level of a fund or sector tends to remain more consistent than its returns. Hence, it is unlikely that your risks will be much greater than the S&P 500 if you stay invested in such a portfolio for the next decade.

The makeup of this portfolio for achieving the highest returns at moderate risk levels from January 1990 through March 1999 were the following sectors of stock indexes:

- 32.5% financial services, brokerage and investment management
- 32.5% computer software and systems
- 15% health care, drugs, and pharmaceuticals
- 20% Asia, excluding Japan

Note that I used S&P stock indexes instead of the best-performing mutual funds, as there wasn't always continuity in funds over the nine-year period and I wanted to isolate the sector effect. Obviously, the best-performing funds in these sectors could have achieved even higher returns. I feel that this portfolio will represent the best strategy for investment returns at moderate risks in the coming decade as well because of the strength of the fundamental trends behind these sectors. Some people might question the Asia portion because of the recent dramatic correction. But that correction was included. And I will show in Chapter 3 why the more-developed regions of Asia, including Hong Kong, South Korea, Singapore, and Taiwan, have very strong demographics in the coming decade and should continue to rebound strongly from the extreme crash in late 1997 and 1998.

In fact, aggressive investors may want to increase the proportion of Asia, excluding Japan, in their portfolios for the coming decade because of the extreme value created in that correction, especially when we see substantial corrections in the future. It is Japan that will continue to see slow growth and even decline during the coming decade, as I will also show in Chapter 3.

Alternate Portfolios for International Sectors

There are many ways that we can change the risks and returns of this investment strategy while still leveraging the most fundamental

2-2. Aggressive Growth Portfolio with Europe
January 1990 through March 1999

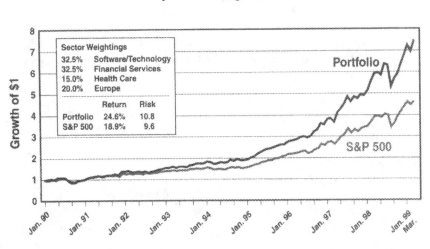

trends for the next decade. The first would be to substitute European large cap stocks for the Asian component of the aggressive portfolio of Chart 2-1 (page 58). Chart 2-2 shows the results of keeping the same balance among financial services, health care, technology, and using European large company stocks instead of Asia for the international component, using the EAFE as the best index to represent the European sector.

The returns were 24.6% and the standard deviation or risk was 10.8%. This portfolio would have produced higher returns than Asia due to the severe Asia crash, but it creates higher risk due to closer correlation rates with the U.S. market. I am projecting that the performance of Europe will be stronger in the coming decade as a result of both demographic trends and the European Union. Therefore, increasing the weighting of European stocks would likely pay off for this portfolio in the future. You may want to split the international part of your portfolio between Asia and Europe or buy a world fund that focuses on those regions.

Another approach to changing the international focus of the portfolio is to eliminate the direct international sectors and include the more stable Dow multinational stocks in the United States, as I have

2-3. Aggressive Growth Portfolio with Domestic Multinational
January 1990 through March 1999

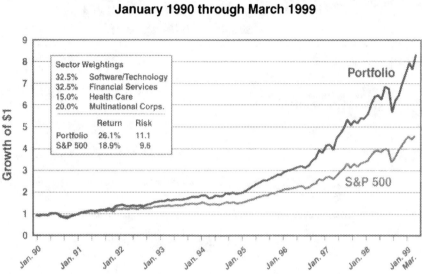

Sector Weightings	
32.5%	Software/Technology
32.5%	Financial Services
15.0%	Health Care
20.0%	Multinational Corps.

	Return	Risk
Portfolio	26.1%	11.1
S&P 500	18.9%	9.6

done in Chart 2-3. The returns here are even higher at 26.1%, but the risk or volatility is higher at 11.1. Here, as an investor, you don't have to expose yourself to the risks of companies outside the United States but can still leverage international growth trends, especially in the emerging countries.

Growth Portfolios with Lower Risks

To lean your portfolio toward a more conservative growth portfolio with higher income, we could add high-income stocks, as I have done in Chart 2-4 (page 62). The standard deviation for this portfolio from January 1990 to March 1999 came in at a similar rate as when adding the Dow, but brought the returns down slightly.

To lower the risk of your portfolio and generate even higher income while maintaining higher-than-average returns, I would suggest increasing the proportion of multinational stocks and adding convertible bonds and fixed-income securities. I chose convertible bonds that have the option for converting into a company's stock at a fixed price,

2-4. Aggressive Growth Portfolio
Substituting High-Income Stocks
January 1990 through March 1999

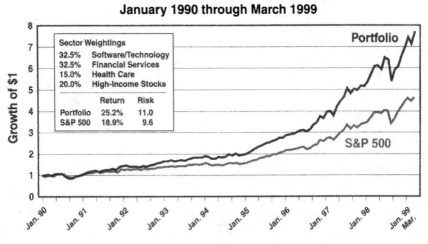

because you still get the positive effects of equity growth. I used prime-rate funds, as they have generated the highest short-term returns for investors and have been less sensitive to falling interest rates. Chart 2-5 shows a portfolio that would have generated returns of 22.3% and beat the S&P 500 by 3.4 percentage points per year, but at the same approximate risk level of 9.7 versus 9.6. This portfolio increased the Dow or multinational weighting to 30% and added prime-rate fixed-income funds to 10% of the portfolio.

If we add 10% in convertible bonds and bring the prime-rate sector up to 30%, then we get a very attractive growth and income portfolio (Chart 2-6). The returns approximately equal the S&P 500 at 18.7%, but the risk and volatility go way down to a standard deviation of 7.0 versus 9.6 on the S&P 500. This portfolio has a 40% income orientation and still equals the S&P 500 in returns since 1990!

For the best conservative portfolio (Chart 2-7, page 64) I brought the prime-rate sector up to 35% and the convertible bonds up to 20%. The Dow, which has very attractive returns at low-risk levels, is 25%, and then I have 10% each of technology and financial services for increasing returns and diversification. This portfolio has a very low risk

2-5. Growth Portfolio
January 1990 through March 1999

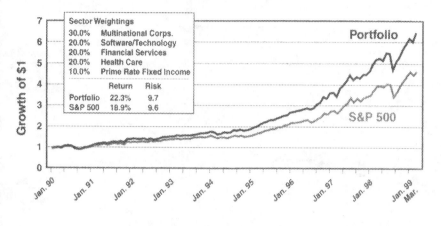

2-6. Growth and Income Portfolio
January 1990 through March 1999

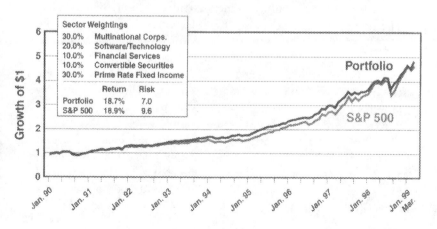

2-7. Conservative Portfolio
January 1990 through March 1999

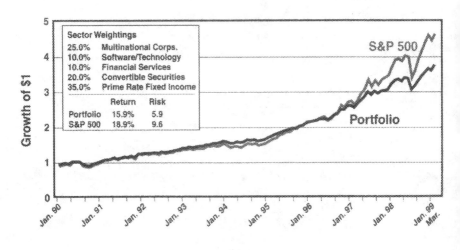

Sector Weightings
25.0%	Multinational Corps.
10.0%	Software/Technology
10.0%	Financial Services
20.0%	Convertible Securities
35.0%	Prime Rate Fixed Income

	Return	Risk
Portfolio	15.9%	5.9
S&P 500	18.9%	9.6

level of 5.9 and still generates very healthy returns at 15.9%, only 3 percentage points lower than the S&P 500. With future returns on the S&P 500 projected to be more like 17%, this portfolio might return something like 13% to 14% with very low risk levels and an income orientation of 55%.

Obviously, past returns are no guarantee of future performance. The returns in these portfolios are all likely to be a bit lower in the next decade than in the past decade. Why? The valuation boom that temporarily stretched returns on the largest company stocks from late 1994 into 1999 will be coming to an end and yields on bonds are forecast by me to be a bit lower. But the risk and volatility levels are likely to remain more in the ranges predicted as past volatility levels have proven to be more predictive of future risk.

These portfolios merely represent starting points for you and/or your advisor to consider how to position your financial assets to leverage the greatest boom in history over the coming decade. There are many alternative portfolios in the aggressive down to conservative risk ranges. To be the most aggressive, you could focus on a portfolio that

2-8. Very Aggressive Portfolio
January 1990 through March 1999

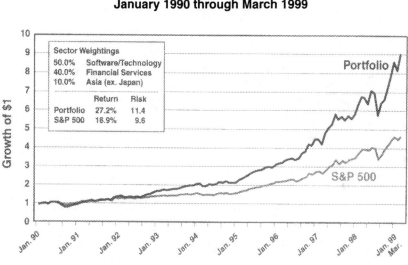

just invested in the very highest return sectors, as in Chart 2-8: 50% in technology, 40% in financial services, and 10% in Asia. That portfolio would have beat the S&P 500 by 8.3 percentage points on average annually and at a cost of a rise in the standard deviation or risk level of only 1.8 to 11.4.

To be the most conservative, you could focus even higher on fixed income and have just 20% in equities and 80% in fixed income, as in Chart 2-9 (page 66). Even with very low risks of 2.8 on the standard deviation, you could still achieve a reasonable return level of 12.5% by including just 10% in technology and 10% in financial services.

The most important point is to sit down now and make sure you consider your wealth and income needs and your ability to tolerate risk and volatility. Allocating into the strongest large cap growth sectors that leverage demographic and technology trends can greatly improve your odds of success in the incredible decade ahead, even in conservative portfolios.

2-9. Very Conservative Portfolio
January 1990 through March 1999

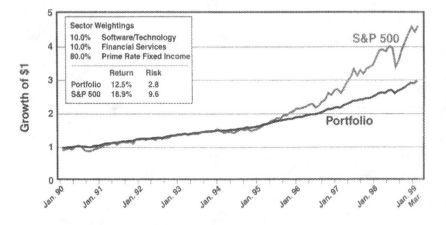

How to Rebalance Your Portfolio
to Take Advantage of Corrections

As I strongly emphasized in *The Roaring 2000s*, the best strategy for almost all investors is to stay invested in such a strong fundamental bull market. It is tempting to think you can take profits after a strong run and wait for the next correction. Or that some new expert has a great timing model. But it would have to be a new expert, as no one has proved capable of doing this consistently over time. Every study I have seen has shown that the more that investors trade, the worse they do. Of course, there are exceptions, and you may be one if your track record proves that to you. Again, have you beat the S&P 500 over five years or more? If not, I would recommend a more systematic approach.

There is a great difference between the capacity for long-term versus short-term forecasting. We as investors should be investing in highly projectable long-term fundamental trends, not in capricious short-term dynamics that are very difficult to predict. Long-term trends are what I call "deterministic" in nature. They are driven by simple cause-and-effect dynamics over time. People spend more money into age 46.5, so we can forecast how long a new generation of consumers will spend increasingly. This is a trend that is almost inevitable, and we can therefore forecast when the economy and stock market will grow, and when it will not, decades in advance. That's the beauty of deterministic forecasting, as I covered in Chapter 1.

It is in the short term that the complexity of change and our economy comes into play, and does it show its stuff! Any single earnings report or the release of an economic indicator by the government or any random political crisis here or around the world can cause stocks to go up or down. These many random factors are too complex for anyone to totally figure out. Therefore, short-term forecasting is not deterministic in nature but "probabilistic." The normal odds of being right in a random situation are the same as for guessing whether a coin will come up heads or tails. And that is 50%. Guessing whether stocks will be up or down today is such a task. Then you add the emotions of fear and greed, and most of our guessing rates are even worse. We tend to sell when we should logically buy, and buy when we should sell. A competent analyst can maybe get up toward 60% or a bit higher. But how do you find such an analyst? And their methods for success come and go, just like the ups and downs of the markets.

Most of us aren't great short-term analysts, and again, the methods of such good analysts don't tend to last long before the market comes up with new tricks. Or we simply don't have the 60 hours a week it would take, even if we had the talent, to be a good short-term analyst. Probabilistic forecasting and short-term trading are more like gambling. And that's what we should do in our leisure time to the degree we like to or can afford it. We shouldn't be managing our economic future or retirement funds in that way.

That doesn't mean we can't leverage corrections in the stock and investment markets. We may not be able to predict corrections reliably, but we can see them when they actually occur. Corrections in the market hit different sectors to different degrees. That creates value for the astute investor. Therefore, the best way to leverage a correction is not to jump out when you think one may occur but to rebalance your portfolio toward the strong long-term sectors based on fundamental deterministic trends that get hit the hardest when such corrections do occur.

For example, let's say you were in the aggressive portfolio in

Chart 2-1 (page 58) originally with 32.5% in technology, 32.5% in financial services, 15% in health care, and 20% in Asia, excluding Japan. In late 1997 Asia was down over 60%! It would make sense to add more of any new money that came available into Asia or to sell a portion of the stronger-performing sectors and buy more of Asia. And, of course, Asia was the strongest sector of that portfolio to rebound after the worldwide correction after late 1998. In the correction from mid-July into early October of 1998, the technology sector was down over 30% versus the S&P 500, which was down only 20%. It would have made sense to add more new money or to make minor shifts toward the technology sector. And that was the domestic sector that performed the best into the stellar rebound from late 1998 into 1999. In early 1999 Latin America, led by the crisis in Brazil, took the largest corrections. That would have been the place to shift more money at that time.

To summarize, the best way to leverage a correction in the market is to switch more from conservative sectors to aggressive and more toward the sectors that get hit the hardest. If you are in various sectors because of strong long-term fundamental trends, then a short-term crisis allows you to buy at greater value and improve your long-term returns. But you don't have to and shouldn't be jumping from cash to stocks every time you or some great analyst thinks there might be a correction. In a strong bull market like this one, the odds are strong that you will miss the next leg up instead of avoiding a brief correction.

In *The Roaring 2000s*, I pointed out that such corrections tend to be very brief in bull markets like 1982 to 2008 or 1942 to 1968. No correction (from the top to the bottom) since 1982 has lasted more than six months. Most have been several weeks or just a few months. And with the exception of 1987, when it took a little over a year and a half to reach new highs, new highs have come within one year and often less. On page 292 of *The Roaring 2000s*, I predicted the correction of 1998 long before it happened. I don't normally focus on predicting corrections, but there is a very reliable four-year political cycle in stocks that I documented in that book.

I ask most investors this question: Even if you had known a correction was very likely, at what point would you have gotten out and when would you have gotten back in? In 1998 the market traded anywhere from 8000 to 9300. Would you have gotten out right at the top, just when many respected analysts thought Dow 10,000 was very likely? And would you have gotten out at the bottom, at a Dow of 7400 on the morning of September 1? Many leading analysts were predicting anywhere from 4500 to 6900 at the time for a bottom. Hewitt Associates, which measures 401K activity, showed a strong spike of investors who switched from stocks to bonds on that day—a very bad decision based on natural human emotions.

The truth is, even if you had known it was coming, your emotions would probably have gotten you out around 8200, when well-known analysts were sounding the alarm, and back in around the same point, when it was pretty clear that the market had reversed back up strongly. The top and the bottom came so fast that it would have been hard to catch anywhere near the top or bottom. That is one of the greatest illusions about corrections and market timing. Even when you are right about anticipating a correction—which few people are—you may make minimal or no gains since you aren't going to pick the exact top or bottom.

Therefore, I don't recommend being out of this market. Stick with the portfolio that you choose yourself, or better with an objective advisor, and leverage corrections by rebalancing toward the more aggressive sectors and/or the highest potential sectors that correct the most. But it also makes sense to periodically rebalance aside from significant corrections.

Periodic Rebalancing

Another principle I covered in *The Roaring 2000s* in Chapter 7 was how to periodically rebalance your portfolio. I give a more detailed example there, but let me just summarize this technique for improving the returns versus the risk of your portfolio. Every one or two years, regardless of corrections, you can simply rebalance your portfolio back to the original target ranges of sector allocation. In the aggressive portfolio in Chart 2-1 (page 58), that would be 32.5% technology, 32.5% financial services, 15% health care, and 20% Asia. As the markets advance, some sectors will perform stronger than other sectors in any one- or two-year period, as technology did in 1999.

That will cause the stronger-performing sectors to become a larger percentage of your portfolio than your original targets. To rebalance, you simply and automatically sell the portion of the stronger sectors and buy the portion of the weaker sectors that will put you back at your original targets. This approach tends to work for the same reason that diversification or asset allocation does. Since different sectors are strong at different times, the strong sectors in the past cycle are increasingly likely to underperform in the next cycle. Periodic rebalancing allows you to take advantage of that principle.

How to Evaluate Mutual Funds, Unit Investment Trusts, and Index Funds

We have seen the emergence of several mutual fund rating services that don't represent the funds but the investor. That is a great innovation. The most prominent include Morningstar, Lipper, and CD Weisenberger. And most business and financial magazines have unbiased mutual fund ratings that likewise take into account risks or volatility and returns, not just overall but compared to the sector that the fund is invested in. These ratings services are a great advance in the financial services industry, but there are some flaws I have noticed in how they rate funds and how we as investors tend to use them.

But let's start by reiterating the advantages these services offer. They are objective and represent the investor, not the funds. They use standard and quantitative systems to evaluate. They measure not only return but risk and the price you pay as an investor for that return. They measure fees and returns net of those fees. They document manager tenure and the turnover or intensity of trading of the fund. They often measure tax efficiency. And they come up with an overall rating for 1-year, 3-year, and 5-year performances, and often 10-year or the life of the fund. These are all very useful indicators. But such ratings systems, like economists, often focus on the trees and miss the forest. And we as investors can end up trading mutual funds just like stocks, which is not what mutual funds were designed for.

The first drawback to such ratings is that they penalize "load" funds. Such funds charge an up-front advisory fee that does not go to the fund but to the advisor who recommended it. No-load funds are not penalized and hence often show slightly better net returns to the investor. But with an advisor you are getting a level of advice that should either improve your performance or take the research and analysis burden off your time and resources. That is value-added and should not be adjusted back into the net returns. You are free to choose to analyze your own investment or delegate that to an advisor for a fair fee.

The more essential drawback is that such ratings systems tend to reward funds and sectors that have outperformed in recent years and may be due for a natural cyclical period of underperformance. Most people buy a fund when it has been upgraded, say, from a four-star to a five-star rating. That is most likely to occur because the sector the fund invests in has had a very positive cycle of performance. That means it is increasingly likely that that sector will start to underperform for the coming year or two. If that does occur, the investor tends to think he or she has made a poor decision and then sells the fund. You can see how that strategy could often put you in the best funds just when they are not performing well. That is not a good investment strategy.

It often makes more sense to buy a fund with a very good long-term track record when it has been downgraded from, say, a five-star to a four-star rating. Such a fund has probably just gone through a difficult cycle in its sector and is increasingly likely to outperform. But here is the catch. You must determine that the fund is positioned in sectors that are likely to continue to outperform or do well on a longer-term basis. Many bond or small cap funds could underperform for the decade to come. Hence, buying them when their ratings get cut back would not be a good strategy.

How to Determine When a Fund Gets Too Big to Continue to Perform Well

The funds that most investors prefer have long-term track records of performance and hence tend to get very large by attracting more investors. Some of these funds continue to outperform, albeit at less advantageous levels, but many increasingly underperform. The reason should be obvious. As one very successful fund manager said: "I started buying stocks I loved. Then as the fund became larger, I had to buy stocks I liked. And then when it became very successful, I had to buy stocks that I didn't hate." The more money you have to invest, the harder it is to buy a stock you like without moving the market and paying more for it. And the harder it is to unload such a stock when you want to without selling at lower prices than you would prefer.

On the other hand, a larger fund can have lower costs in overhead, research, and transaction costs due to the simple economies of scale in business. Research shows that funds that reach a critical mass of economies of scale in the $100 million to $500 million range do best when they are strong performers. But such funds often have too short a track record to make us feel confident as investors. How do we resolve this dilemma of size versus track record?

I have come up with an indicator that can help based on one of the best measures of risk versus return. That is the Sharpe ratio. This indicator attempts to measure the differential between the higher returns generated above average by an investment manager versus the higher risks experienced above average to achieve those returns. Think of it as the incremental returns versus the incremental risk. Most rating services use the Sharpe ratio as an indicator for the relative performance of mutual funds and investment managers. But this ratio is typically featured only in the present year or over past time periods at best. The real secret is measuring the Sharpe ratio **over time.**

If a fund can grow in assets and continue to improve or at least sustain its Sharpe ratio, that is a sign that the fund or investment manager is getting better at managing risks versus returns over time, despite the disadvantages of scale. Most of the greatest funds have had improving Sharpe ratios over time even as they got larger. But many of these funds have seen their Sharpe ratios start to flatten out. That is the first sign that a fund may start to underperform compared to its past track record. But the time to consider moving out of a fund is when the Sharpe ratio starts to fall, especially for more than one or two years.

Therefore, I advise sticking with strong funds with good longterm track records until their Sharpe ratios start to flatten and decline. Look at the Sharpe ratio over 1 year, 3 years, 5 years, and even 10 years, if available, and start to question a great fund when it starts to plateau and decline. It is inevitable that the Sharpe ratio may slow in its advance for a good fund as it grows. You are trading off the security of a long-term track record for a new fund that may be hot and then cold. But when it starts to plateau or decline, you should question the fund and look for new funds in that sector that are smaller and showing rising Sharpe ratios over time.

A New Look at Risk and Volatility

I have had the pleasure of working with Rodney Johnson, an investment analyst at 1-800-MUTUALS and Heritage Capital, a private investment fund. He introduced me to a different view on risk and volatility. Yes, the more volatile the returns of a fund, the more ups and downs it would seem that you would have to experience as an investor. And most of us don't want higher risk and volatility. That is what turns many of the best performance funds into a liability for us investors. We love them when they are hot, and they do tend to outperform over time. But they scare us into selling, and hence underperforming, when they go down to greater extremes than the markets in corrections. Then they race up without us into the next great bull market.

But there is an important difference. Think about stocks like Microsoft or Dell. They have appreciated at very high rates over time and suffered substantial setbacks at times. But the truth is they go up far more than they go down. The traditional measures of risk and volatility, like standard deviation and beta, which track the deviation from the long-term trends in the S&P or in the respective indexes of those sectors, would often say that such stocks have high volatility. But most of that volatility is on the upside of those indexes, not on the downside, as these are very consistent outperformers due to superior business and management strategies that they have been able to sustain over long periods.

How many investors would object to a stock or fund that tends to greatly outperform on the upside but doesn't tend to underperform on the downside when there are corrections in the markets or in that sector? But standard measures of volatility would penalize such a stock or fund because of its upside outperformance and volatility. Rodney Johnson came up with an indicator that helps differentiate between positive volatility and negative volatility. He starts by looking at the range of returns negative and positive over any time frame, especially over 3-year, 5-year, and 10-year time frames. In addition to average returns and risks, you look at the maximum returns a stock or fund would have achieved over the time period you are measuring versus the lowest returns, including negative.

This gives you a high and low range, which lets you feel how it would have been to actually own such a stock or fund over that time period. What would have been the greatest returns and the worst returns you would have experienced year to year or quarter to quarter? You can create even greater insight by measuring the difference between the highest returns above the average of that sector versus the lowest returns below the average of that sector. The ratio of the upside returns to the downside will give you a rough-cut feel for whether the fund tends toward positive or negative volatility, but only at the extremes.

To get a more accurate gauge of whether a fund is likely to have more upside or downside potential over time versus the S&P 500 or any other benchmark index, you can use the Johnson Indicator. Here is the formula for any period you want to use (three years or longer recommended) with simple data you can get from Morningstar or any rating service:

1. (Average Annual Fund Return **Plus** Fund Standard Deviation) **Minus** S&P 500 Average Return **Divided** (In total) **By** Fund Standard Deviation

   Minus

2. S&P 500 Average Return **Minus** (Average Fund Return **Minus** Fund Standard Deviation) **Divided** (In total) **By** S&P 500 Standard Deviation

   Equals: The Johnson Indicator (positive or negative)

If the indicator is positive, then that is a good indicator of higher chances of upside volatility rather than down. And, of course, a negative indicator is not a good sign. The higher the positive indicator, the better, and vice versa for the negative side. Here is an example:

	S&P 500	Fund
3-Year Average Return	18.86%	26.12%
Standard Deviation (3 years)	9.60	11.12

1. [(26.12 + 11.12) – 18.86]/11.12
   (37.24 – 18.86)/11.12 = 18.38/11.12 = **1.65**

Minus

2. [18.86 – (26.12 – 11.12)]/9.60
   (18.86 – 15.00)/9.60 = 3.86/9.60 = **0.40**

   1.65 – 0.40 = 1.25 (positive)

In this case, the fund had a mildly positive indicator, which is a good sign. It is most helpful to calculate this over 3-year, 5-year, and 10-year periods, if possible, to ascertain whether this is a long-term trend or not. It would be even better to compare a fund to an index that represents that sector instead of just using the S&P 500—like the Russell 2000 for a small cap fund, or the S&P 500 technology index for a technology fund.

Style Consistency of Funds

I have emphasized the importance of combining different asset classes or sectors of investments for building a portfolio that should increase the likelihood that you can achieve greater returns at lower risks by bringing together different sectors that move in different or low-correlating patterns over time. But you can't do this unless the fund managers stick to their knitting! If fund managers chase different sectors of investments, from stocks to bonds or large cap to small cap or technology to financial services, to achieve the highest returns, then you can't rely on those sectors for effective diversification effects and you can't as reliably plan your future. So look for funds that have a consistent style or asset/sector focus over time. Many of the rating services measure this as well.

There is another reason that you want to see style consistency. You can't expect a fund manager to be able to understand and master all sectors of our economy. We need them to be specialists. By specializing on a sector, they can create better returns versus risk if they know what they are doing. It should be the task of the investment funds to specialize on certain sectors, acting as "servers," and to allow us or our financial advisors, acting as "browsers," to decide which sectors we need to combine in our portfolios to meet our individualized needs.

The exception would be a small but growing number of funds that use an asset allocation strategy of combining a number of key sectors for achieving the best risk/return ratios and then rebalance strategically or periodically, as I have prescribed for the best risk/returns ratios as an overall strategy. These funds are classified as asset allocation funds. Such funds are looking to create a broad investment strategy rather than a sector-only strategy and can represent a viable one-stop approach for the investor. But such funds should employ specialists in each sector to leverage the benefits of specialization in investment knowledge.

Now that I have looked at the portfolio strategies for leveraging the greatest boom in history, I will take a closer look at the frontier of investing. I also expect the best international markets to outperform the S&P 500 in the next decade. And as I have pointed out in this chapter, they provide excellent diversification in your portfolio. But just as in domestic markets, you must understand the fundamental trends in other countries you are considering investing in. Most of the rest of the world had strong baby booms after World War II and hence have strong growth prospects. But there are some extreme exceptions, like Japan. I will look not only at demographic trends in all the key countries around the world in Part 2, but also at the technological infrastructures that will be critical to growth and productivity in the Roaring 2000s.

PART 2

Opportunities
Around the Globe

CHAPTER 3

International Demographic and Technology Trends in Developed Countries

IN THIS CHAPTER I will look at the demographic and generation patterns driving most of the countries of significance and interest in the developed world, where most of us are more comfortable investing. But first I would like to review the differences between using demographics to project economic trends in the United States and using them for other developed countries. Most countries have a smaller internal marketplace than the United States does, and place a much greater emphasis on specialization of industries and trade with other countries. Developed nations with significant export economies, from Japan to Germany to Australia, depend on the competitiveness of such industries and on government support. The age demographics within the country, therefore, drive only its own internal consumer economy. Export economies are more dependent on the age demographics and generation trends in the countries they export to, as well as their competitiveness in export industries.

In the U.S. market, trade with other countries is small compared to the overall economy. Exports make up only 12% of our GDP. Hence, the spending wave or generation spending model works very well in projecting the U.S. economy and stock market. It is a bigger part of other developed-country economies, but not the whole picture. Nevertheless, I predicted the dramatic collapse in Japan before it happened in the late 1980s based primarily on a downturn in spending of a generation born before World War II, out of cycle with most of the rest of the developed world. I have been predicting for over a decade that most European countries would boom later and follow the demographic trends in the United States because of a smaller and slightly later baby boom after World War II. And now that is happening as well. So demographics still represent a useful tool for projecting the relative growth potential of developed countries around the world.

It is also important, in judging the potential for productivity as well as competitiveness in export industries, to look at the technological infrastructures of each country. To what degree do consumers and workers have access to modern communications and media to advance their skills and access to information? After all, we are in the greatest information revolution in history, the first since the printing press and scientific revolution in the late 1400s to 1500s. Therefore, a country's information infrastructure is the other critical factor for judging its long-term growth potential. I am going to use "The Wired World Atlas," published in the November 1998 issue of *Wired* magazine. It is the best summary of total information and media infrastructures I have seen.

Wired looks at the penetration of phone lines, TVs, Internet hosts, cell phones, radios, PCs, satellite dishes, and cable—what they call "The Media Spectrum." They rate every country, developed and developing, from 1 to 192 in overall rankings of combined infrastructure development. I have simply converted their ratings to a 1 to 20 scale, with 1 being the most developed infrastructure (example, United States) and 20 being the least developed (example, Niger).

Most countries around the world had a massive baby boom just before and after World War II. But different countries had baby booms on slightly different time frames and to different degrees. There are exceptions, the biggest being Japan. Let me start by using age demographics to demonstrate why Japan has been in an economic slump and a bear market in stocks ever since early 1990.

Why Japan's Economy Is So Weak

If we look at Japan's birth index in Chart 3-1, we can see how we could have seen two important economic events well in advance.

3-1. Japan Birth Index
47-Year Birth Lag

Source: Japanese Ministry of Health and Welfare.

Japan's births were generally up until 1943. Like most developed countries around the world, Japan had a sharp drop in births during World War II. From 1944 to 1946, births dropped dramatically in Japan, even more than in most countries. If you look at the second line below the chart, I have converted the time line to a 47-year lag for peak in spending. That drop-off in births during World War II caused an economic slowdown in Japan in the early '90s, from 1990 to 1992, as occurred in many countries around the world. I forecast the bursting of Japan's asset and stock bubble (and a recession in the United States) in late 1989 based on this simple principle of age demographics. Japan's bubble burst from early 1990 into mid-1992 as their stock market dropped by 67%, from a high of 38,900 in January 1990 to 14,500 in April 1992. You could have seen that coming while most economists were praising Japan's economic miracle and government/business alliance in the late 1980s.

As in Asia in the 1990s, Japan's government had favored key

industries through a top-down economic model (doomed to fail in a bottoms-up information age). They provided debt from government-controlled banks at very low rates of interest to the point that their key industries greatly overexpanded. The low-cost money and protectionism leveraged stock and real estate values to extremes that would not be allowed in a free-market economy like that in the United States. The more stock and real estate prices rose, the cheaper it was for such companies to raise more capital and expand, despite low returns on equity compared to U.S. corporations. Such expansion led to higher stock and real estate prices. In 1989 Japan's stock market was worth much more than the entire U.S. stock market. Real estate in Tokyo was worth much more than all the real estate in the United States. This was a classic "bubble economy." It only took a sharp slowdown in 1990 from the dip in births during World War II to burst that bubble.

As you can see, like most countries, Japan had a strong surge in births after World War II, from 1947 into 1950, when the soldiers came home. That caused the Japanese economy to rebound after 1992 into 1996, but at a lower rate because of the incredible devastation from the bursting of the economic bubble and the collapse of the banking system due to bad loans to corporations and real estate speculation. But then the real recession started in late 1996 and early 1997. Japan had a steep decline in births, or a baby bust, between 1950 and 1957, the very years when most countries, including the United States, had their largest baby booms. That means a dramatic slowdown in consumer spending from 1997 into 2004 on a 47-year lag for the peak in spending, as is reflected in the lower scale of the time axis using a 47-year birth lag! And that is what we are seeing.

The point is that Japan will not recover fully even as the rest of Asia does, although the recovery of Asia from the 1997–98 crisis will help Japan's export industries, as will the continuing strength of the rest of the world. The sluggishness of Japan's economy into 2004 will cause off and on problems in Asia. But note that Asia boomed after the 1990–91 recession despite the continued slowdown in Japan's economy and its stock market into 1992. Therefore, I am still very bullish on the rest of Asia in the coming decade and even beyond, as I will show in the sections on Asia in this chapter and in Chapter 4 on emerging countries. I am not recommending that you invest in Japan in the coming decade, although there may be substantial rebounds in its stock market at times. Conversely, Japan will be a good country to invest in from 2008–9 into 2020, when its next generation is on a spending and productivity rise and the United States and many countries are in a down trend. As in the 1970s, Japan represents a great countertrend investment for equities and stocks for our portfolios. The sector that should be the strongest in the present period of innovation and change would be small company stocks.

Looking at Demographic Trends in the Developed World

In each country or region I will first look at the growth potential from new generations moving into their peak years of spending and productivity, around age 46.5. Note that in using age demographics to gauge future growth potential by country, I am going to take a different approach than I did with the United States in Chapter 1. There I added immigration (after adjusting for age) to the birth index and projected forward 46.5 years for the average family's peak in spending. Here I am going to take a shortcut. I will use an age distribution chart (in five-year groupings) by country, which is easier to obtain uniformly from the United Nations and has the added advantage of already including immigration. But the trick here is that you have to read these charts backward from the peak age of spending (the age 45–49 group) toward the peak age bar, or cohort, of the younger generation bulge coming into that peak in future years. This will tell you how steep the growth curve (or decline) will be ahead and about how long the economy will grow before reaching a downward trend in spending and productivity. The age distribution charts used are as of 1995, not 1999.

Let's start with the developed European countries, which are characterized largely by more mature economies and generation patterns, but place more emphasis on export-led growth than the United States does. In the mid-1990s European stock markets started to surge and actually outperformed the U.S. market in 1997. I expect European stock markets to continue to do well in the coming decade. But I would be surprised if those markets actually outperformed the U.S. market over the coming decade. The performance should be close and represents a good diversification strategy for the larger portion of our U.S. portfolios.

European Markets

As monetary union has become a reality and companies are finally facing stronger pressures to re-engineer, downsize, and merge as U.S. companies have in the past decade, profits in Europe have been accelerating. The generation demographics in Europe will be generally favorable over the coming decade and even a bit beyond because of a smaller but slightly later baby boom in many countries. But remember that, like Japan, these smaller, highly industrialized nations are far more dependent upon exports than the U.S. economy. So the leading companies that have been rallying in recent years are also benefiting from worldwide growth beyond their own consumer spending demographics, much as the large multinational brand leaders in the United States and Canada have. Let's start by looking at the age demographics in western Europe, the core of the economy there.

In Chart 3-2 we start with the age 45–49 cohort and note that the spending tide will rise for about 15 years from 1995 (or three cohorts of 5 years each) as we move backward into the peak cohort at age 30–34. In other words, the peak of the baby boom generation in western Europe as of 1995 was age 30–34 in 1995. And these young consumers will spend increasingly into their peak around age 45–49 for 15 years after 1995, or into about 2010. That means the economy should be in a growth phase in spending into about 2010 and that there shouldn't be a steep falloff until around 2015, 20 years after the 20–24 cohort, at which the age groups decline more rapidly. This means that the economies in western Europe will be more buoyant at first than the U.S. economy after the peak here in 2008–9.

Though not quite as strong as the United States in the next decade, the western European countries as a block will boom about two to five years longer than the United States and Canada. Notice, though, like Canada (in the section on North America) but even worse, there is no echo baby boom (you may want to refer ahead to Charts 3-34 and 3-35 [page 106] for the United States and Canada for comparison). This means Europe will really lose ground in growth after 2015 and have no substantial echo boom into the 2040s, like the United States. Germany (Chart 3-3) is one of the stars here, with higher

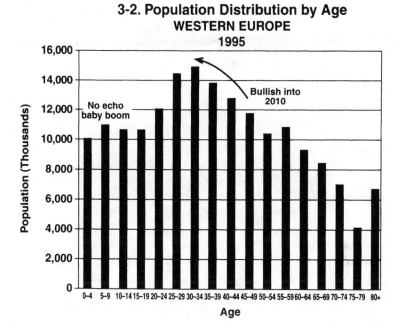

3-2. Population Distribution by Age
WESTERN EUROPE
1995

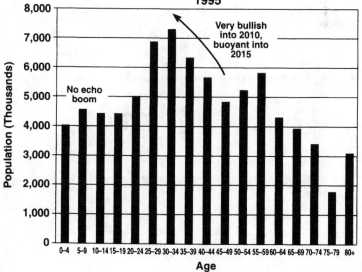

3-3. Population Distribution by Age
GERMANY
1995

immigration rates, which gives them the strongest baby boom generation wave, which should peak around 2010 to 2012. Germany's information infrastructure index rates 19 on a scale of 20, but the higher
wage rates make Germany less competitive.

Switzerland (Chart 3-4) and Austria (Chart 3-5) also look strong
for the next 12 to 15 years, just as Germany does, due to higher immigration rates. Switzerland rates 20 on the information index, just behind the United States in *Wired*'s survey. Austria rates 19, much like
Germany. France (Chart 3-6) has only flat to very moderate growth demographics from now through the next 25 years, into about 2020 to
2023. But France will have the most stable demographics when the
next global downturn begins in the United States and many other
countries after 2009. Such a flat demographic outlook means that export growth and measures to stimulate productivity are essential over
the next decade. France has a rating of 19 on information infrastructures. However, the French government and culture have an antipro-

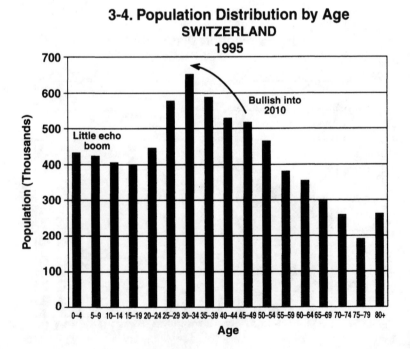

3-4. Population Distribution by Age
SWITZERLAND
1995

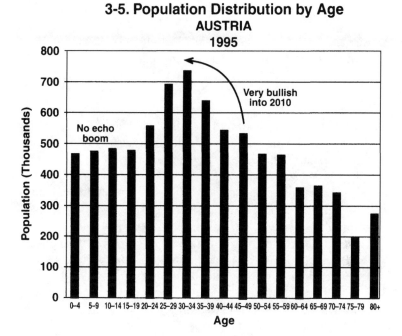

3-5. Population Distribution by Age
AUSTRIA
1995

No echo boom

Very bullish into 2010

Population (Thousands)

Age

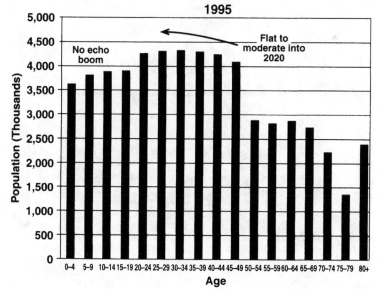

3-6. Population Distribution by Age
FRANCE
1995

No echo boom

Flat to moderate into 2020

Population (Thousands)

Age

gressive and very protectionist stance, which should make its transition to the European Union difficult at first, much like Canada in the early years of NAFTA. France would not be my top choice for investments in the coming years.

Belgium (Chart 3-7) and the Netherlands (Chart 3-8) look more like Great Britain (see Chart 3-14, page 92), with moderately booming demographics over the next 15 years. Belgium scores 18 on information infrastructures, while the Netherlands scores a strong 19.

To summarize, western Europe looks strong for the coming decade because of favorable demographics, very good information infrastructures, and the movement toward European union.

The real weakness in demographics is in northern Europe (Chart 3-9), largely in the Scandinavian countries. Sweden (Chart 3-10, page 90) and Finland (Chart 3-11, page 90) have falling spending waves over the next decade, with Finland bearish into 2020. Norway (Chart 3-12, page 91) has a very moderate rise in spending due over the next 20 years. Here a strong export economy and a strong embrace of new

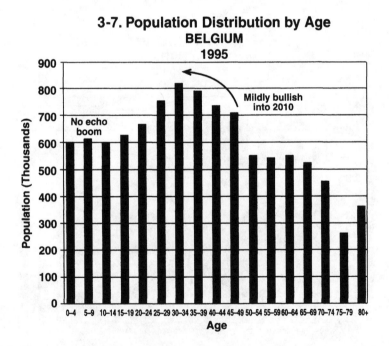

3-7. Population Distribution by Age
BELGIUM
1995

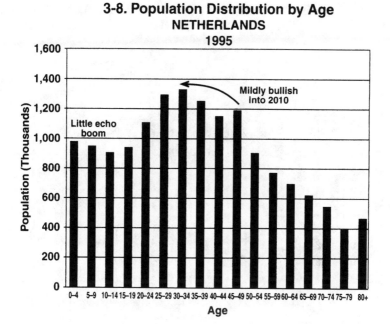

3-8. Population Distribution by Age
NETHERLANDS
1995

Little echo boom

Mildly bullish into 2010

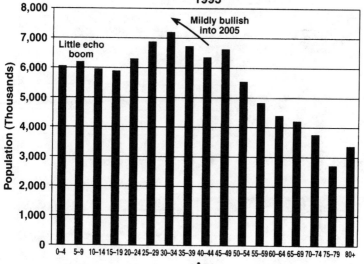

3-9. Population Distribution by Age
NORTHERN EUROPE
1995

Little echo boom

Mildly bullish into 2005

3-10. Population Distribution by Age
SWEDEN
1995

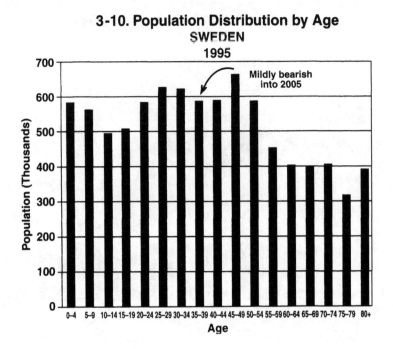

3-11. Population Distribution by Age
FINLAND
1995

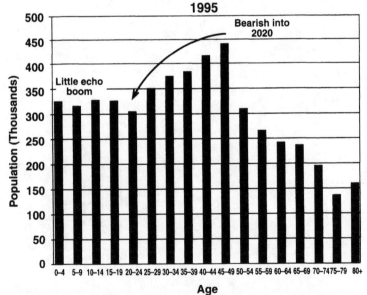

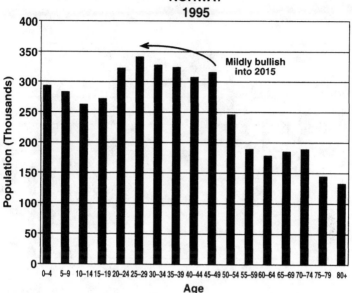

3-12. Population Distribution by Age
NORWAY
1995

Mildly bullish
into 2015

Population (Thousands)

Age

technologies will be needed even more to sustain any type of reasonable growth rates.

Denmark (Chart 3-13, page 92) also has mildly declining trends into around 2005. The Scandinavian countries have their greatest strength in information technologies. Not only do companies from Nokia to Ericsson have commanding leads in cellular phone and wireless technologies, but the overall ratings in penetration rates of information infrastructures are very high. Sweden and Denmark rate 20, Norway rates 19, and Finland rates 17. Overall, Scandinavia rates a very mild bullish indicator for investment, weak on demographics, strong on information technologies.

Great Britain (Chart 3-14, page 92) has moderately rising demographics over the coming 10 to 15 years before falling off strongly around 2012 to 2014. Ireland (Chart 3-15, page 93) has relatively flat demographics into around 2010 and then a strong upsurge into 2025, which will make it a good "depression" play for business and investments, along with France, after 2009. Great Britain rates 19 on the information index, while Ireland rates 17.

Southern Europe (Chart 3-16, page 93) has strong demographics

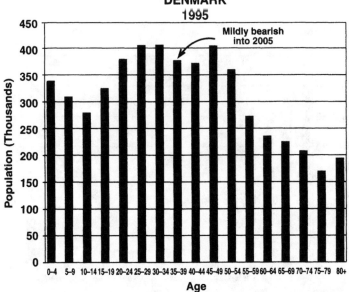

3-13. Population Distribution by Age
DENMARK
1995

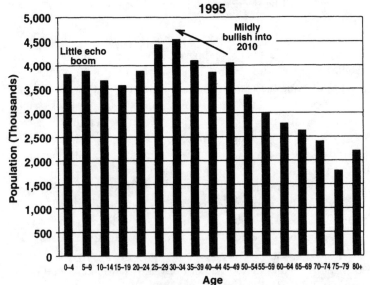

3-14. Population Distribution by Age
GREAT BRITAIN
1995

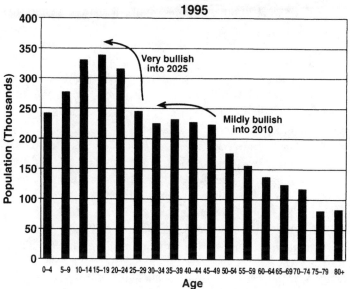

3-15. Population Distribution by Age
IRELAND
1995

Population (Thousands)

Very bullish
into 2025

Mildly bullish
into 2010

Age

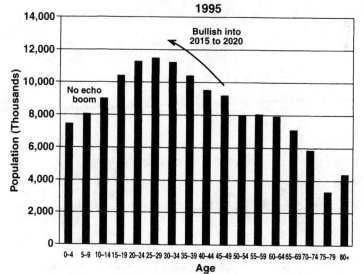

3-16. Population Distribution by Age
SOUTHERN EUROPE
1995

Population (Thousands)

Bullish into
2015 to 2020

No echo
boom

Age

rising into 2018 to 2020 but a little less dramatic than in western Europe. Italy (Chart 3-17) has strong trends into 2015, and its rating on the information index is 17. Spain is the real rising star of Europe (Chart 3-18), with the strongest demographic trends over the next 15 years. Spain also has very favorable trends toward free-market policies in government. It also rates a pretty strong 17 on the information index. I would rate this country as having the strongest investment potential in the coming decade and beyond in Europe. Portugal (Chart 3-19) has a more moderate rise in demographic trends, with especially strong rises from 2015 to 2020, another great depression play. Portugal also rates 17 on the information index. Greece (Chart 3-20, page 96) has milder rising-growth prospects into 2015 but rates a strong 18 on the information index. Overall, southern Europe looks positive but not as strong as western Europe, with the exception of Spain and perhaps northern Italy (due to its strong entrepreneurial revolution).

Eastern Europe has a somewhat different generation cycle from

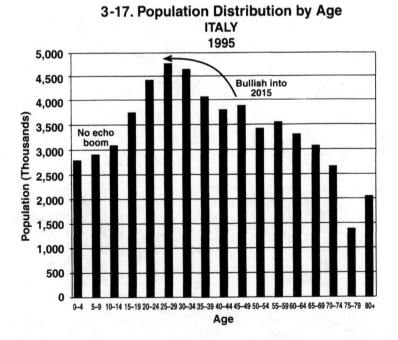

3-17. Population Distribution by Age
ITALY
1995

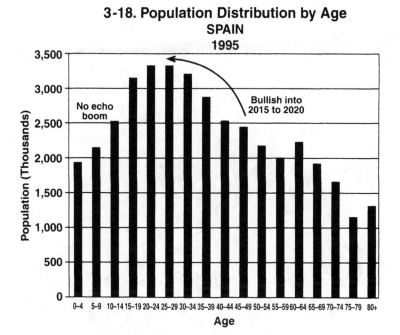

3-18. Population Distribution by Age
SPAIN
1995

No echo boom

Bullish into 2015 to 2020

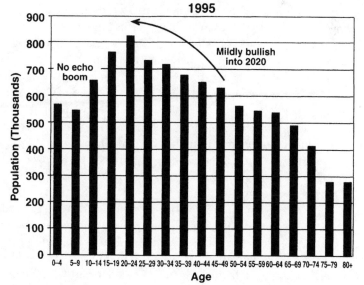

3-19. Population Distribution by Age
PORTUGAL
1995

No echo boom

Mildly bullish into 2020

3-20. Population Distribution by Age
GREECE
1995

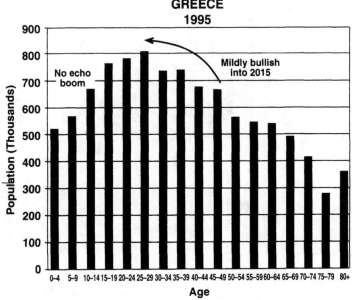

the rest of Europe. As you can see in Chart 3-21, overall demographic trends there should peak even earlier than in the United States, by 2005. Hungary (Chart 3-22) has been one of the best-performing countries in the region, but its spending trends should be peaking by around 2000 and then will turn down sharply for 10 years while the rest of the world is booming. It rates 15 on the information index. Czechoslovakia (Chart 3-23, page 98) has had declining numbers of people moving into peak spending since around 1995 and will see its demographic trends bottom around 2015. It also rates 15 on information technologies. The Czech economy has remained stronger than you would expect, due to its strong entrepreneurial trends.

Poland's demographics (Chart 3-24, page 98) will peak by around 2005. Growth will slow from 2000 to 2005, and then downward trends will occur into around 2015. Poland rates only 13 on the information index. Romania (Chart 3-25, page 99) will see slowing spending growth from demographics into around 2010, then an upsurge, and its information rating is only 12. In the Russian Federation (Chart 3-26, page 99)

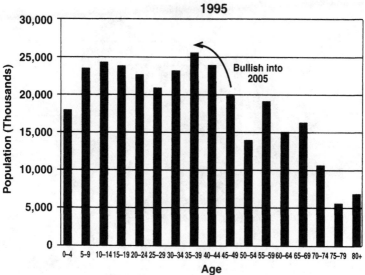

3-21. Population Distribution by Age
EASTERN EUROPE
1995

Bullish into
2005

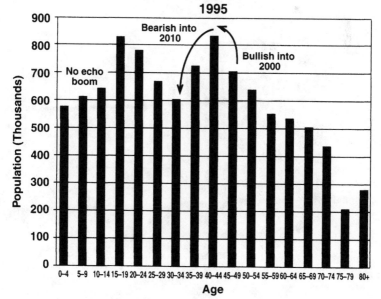

3-22. Population Distribution by Age
HUNGARY
1995

Bearish into
2010

Bullish into
2000

No echo
boom

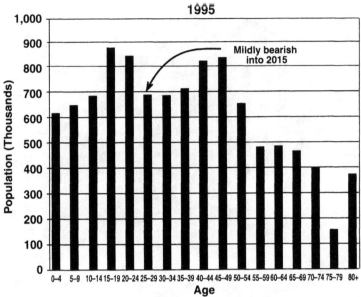

3-23. Population Distribution by Age
CZECH REPUBLIC
1995

Mildly bearish
into 2015

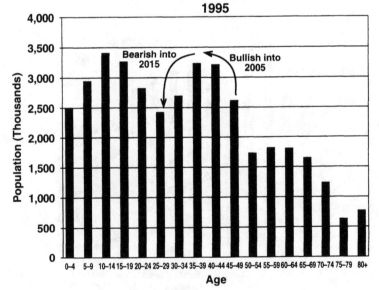

3-24. Population Distribution by Age
POLAND
1995

Bearish into
2015

Bullish into
2005

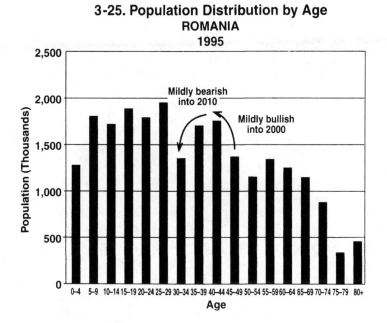

3-25. Population Distribution by Age
ROMANIA
1995

Mildly bearish
into 2010

Mildly bullish
into 2000

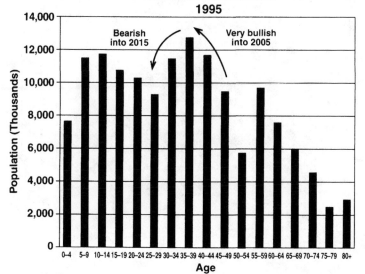

3-26. Population Distribution by Age
RUSSIAN FEDERATION
1995

Bearish
into 2015

Very bullish
into 2005

trends should be up into around 2005 and then down into 2015. The
trends will be similar but slightly less bullish in Ukraine (Chart
3-27). Ukraine and Russia rate 13 on the information index.

Turkey is not technically considered part of eastern Europe in
United Nations data but is often grouped there. It has dramatically
different demographics (Chart 3-28). Turkey looks more like a newly
emerging third world country with the early beginnings of a generation bulge, but with a peak in the younger years of 10–14 and
15–19. But I am going to include it here, not in the next chapter.
Demographic trends should be the most bullish in Turkey into
around 2030. The biggest reason for including Turkey with the
more-developed countries of Europe is its strong technological rating
of 14. I would rate this as another opportune country to consider for
investment.

To summarize, European economies look mostly strong over the
coming decade, and many countries will have favorable demographics
2 to 5 and even up to 10 years after the U.S., Canadian, Australian,

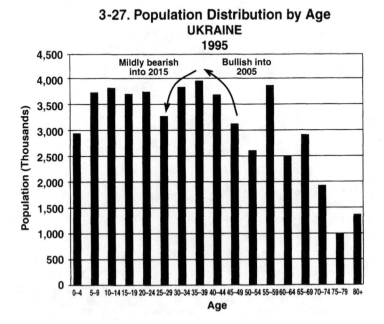

3-27. Population Distribution by Age
UKRAINE
1995

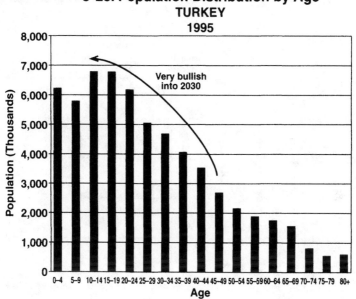

**3-28. Population Distribution by Age
TURKEY
1995**

New Zealand, and Hong Kong baby booms peak. It has strong potential, plus the European Economic Union is finally moving forward with the common currency for 1999. But there are real questions as to whether the average worker, particularly in countries like France, will accept the layoffs and industry mergers and relocations that will be accelerated in the next few years. Expect some turbulence following the Euro in select countries, and look to buy large cap multinational European companies and mutual funds over the coming years as well, especially in corrections in those markets.

Asian Markets

Chart 3-29 (page 102) shows the age distribution for Japan and its very different generation bulges versus the United States, as I described in detail at the beginning of this chapter. It was the only major developed country not to have a baby boom after World War II. Checking the age cohort of 45–49 in the Japan chart, you can see that the last generation

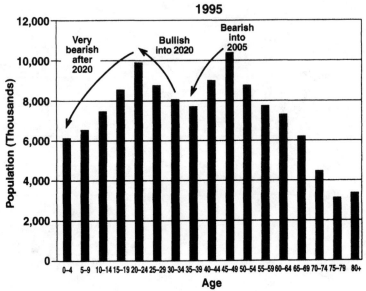

3-29. Population Distribution by Age
JAPAN
1995

bulge is now past its peak spending years of around 47 as of 1995. The Japanese economy should be weak internally from consumer spending into about 2005 to 2008. The next generation peak is at age 20–24. They will drive a consumer-led boom from around 2005 into 2020. Japan rates only an 18 on the information index, well behind the United States and the best-developed countries, another reason to avoid investments in Japan outside the best multinational companies positioned to compete overseas.

Let's contrast Japan with Hong Kong and the more-developed "Tiger" countries in Asia. Hong Kong (Chart 3-30) has a dramatic baby boom generation very close in line with the United States, and it should peak in its spending between 2008 and 2010. Hong Kong rates a very strong 19 on the information index. I rated Hong Kong a very strong buy signal back in early 1998, between 6500 and 8500, for these reasons. Macau's (Chart 3-31) very bullish baby boom will peak earlier, by 2005, and see a more dramatic downturn in consumer spending into 2025. It rates only 16 on the information index.

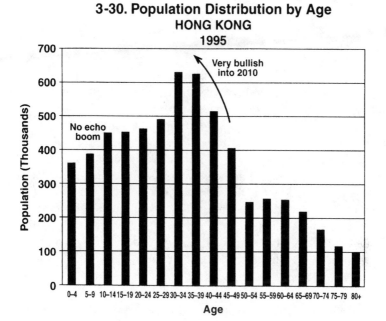

3-30. Population Distribution by Age
HONG KONG
1995

Population (Thousands)

No echo boom

Very bullish into 2010

Age: 0–4 5–9 10–14 15–19 20–24 25–29 30–34 35–39 40–44 45–49 50–54 55–59 60–64 65–69 70–74 75–79 80+

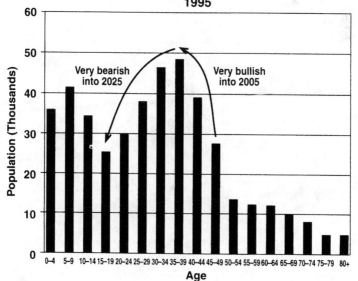

3-31. Population Distribution by Age
MACAU
1995

Population (Thousands)

Very bearish into 2025

Very bullish into 2005

Age: 0–4 5–9 10–14 15–19 20–24 25–29 30–34 35–39 40–44 45–49 50–54 55–59 60–64 65–69 70–74 75–79 80+

Singapore's age demographics (Chart 3-32) are like Hong Kong's, very positive into around 2010, then with a strong drop-off. Singapore also rates a strong 19 on the information index and is perhaps the technological model for Asia. It is making the greatest investments for the future, although such government-led investments can be overdone at times. South Korea (Chart 3-33) has the most bullish chart for the coming decade and even for the decade beyond, into around 2020. South Korea will be a strong country in the next global downturn along with Japan, and it rates a fairly strong 17 on information technologies. It has rebounded the strongest from the 1998 correction. Taiwan is the other more-developed Tiger country in Asia that has positive age demographics into at least the next decade, but the United Nations database does not have age demographics for Taiwan. Taiwan rates a very strong 18 on the information index and has strong potential for the coming decade.

To summarize, I am very bullish on the more-developed Tiger countries in Asia over the coming decade and beyond. Since these stock markets are more volatile than the U.S. and European markets, I

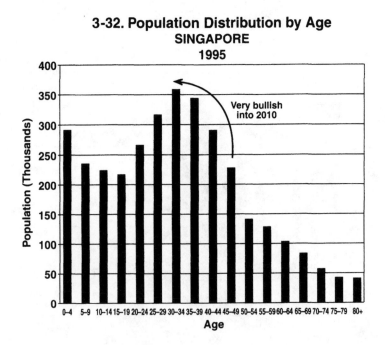

3-32. Population Distribution by Age
SINGAPORE
1995

3-33. Population Distribution by Age
REPUBLIC OF KOREA
1995

Very bullish
into 2020

(Y-axis: Population (Thousands), 0 to 5,000 in 500 increments)

(X-axis: Age — 0–4, 5–9, 10–14, 15–19, 20–24, 25–29, 30–34, 35–39, 40–44, 45–49, 50–54, 55–59, 60–64, 65–69, 70–74, 75–79, 80+)

recommend buying these countries on strong corrections to protect yourself from the downside volatility. The last such opportunities came in early and late 1998 and could come again in late 1999. We may see more buy opportunities in the coming years from setbacks due to weakness in Japan or from the volatile and emerging political structures in the developing countries in Asia (discussed in the next chapter).

North America

Even though I looked in depth at U.S. trends in Chapter 1 and beyond, let's compare the five-year age demographics of the United States to the rest of the world. Chart 3-34 (page 106) shows the strong trend up into around 2005 to 2010 and then a more pronounced falloff in spending than in many other developed countries. Canada (Chart 3-35, page 106) has a very similar baby boom and baby bust, with slightly more dramatic growth between 2004 and 2008 due to strong immigration and births in British Columbia. But Canada has no significant echo baby boom to follow, except in British Columbia and Alberta, where the future of Canada's growth clearly lies. The absence of an echo baby

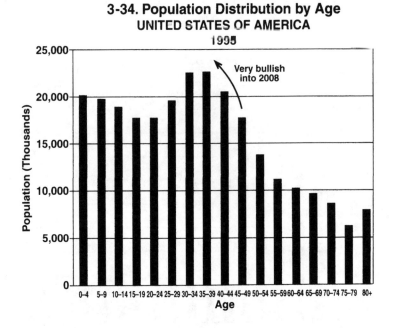

3-34. Population Distribution by Age
UNITED STATES OF AMERICA
1995

Very bullish into 2008

Population (Thousands) vs *Age*

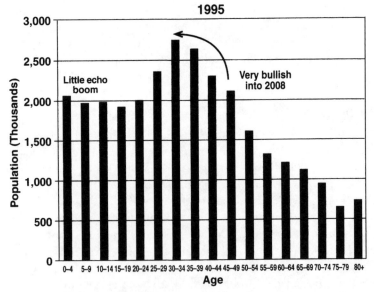

3-35. Population Distribution by Age
CANADA
1995

Little echo boom

Very bullish into 2008

Population (Thousands) vs *Age*

boom not only weakens the growth potential way out from 2020 into 2040 but means lower family formation in the decade ahead, which is also a stimulant to spending and economic growth.

The United States and Canada both boast the highest information-technology indexes, at a rating of 20, with the United States being slightly stronger. All English-speaking countries will have an advantage in the information age at first. And Mexico's younger age distribution provides a needed balance to the aging trends in the United States and Canada, as I will show in Chapter 4. Overall, North America should exhibit slightly higher growth rates than Europe in the coming decade, but a sharper and earlier downturn by 2009. North America should continue to provide the best overall risk-adjusted returns for investors into 2008.

Australia/New Zealand

Australia (Chart 3-36) has a very similar baby boom to the United States into about 2008, although the growth in the coming decade should not

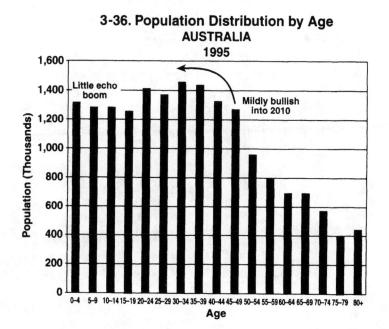

3-36. Population Distribution by Age
AUSTRALIA
1995

be quite as strong. But it has a longer tail of births and immigration, which will cause its economy to be more buoyant into 2019 or 2020 before falling off, with no echo baby boom to fuel the next wave of growth. New Zealand's age demographics (Chart 3-37) are similar but will be more moderate in growth in the coming decade, with better buoyancy out into 2020. Australia rates a strong 19 on the information index, and New Zealand rates on the high end of the 18 side of the index. Both of these countries will benefit from their English-speaking side of the software standard on the Internet.

Summary

There will be growth in most countries around the world in the incredible decade ahead. Chart 3-38 shows the top 10 in demographic growth potential. The fastest growth in the developed world will still tend to be in the United States and the Asian Tigers, with parts of Eu-

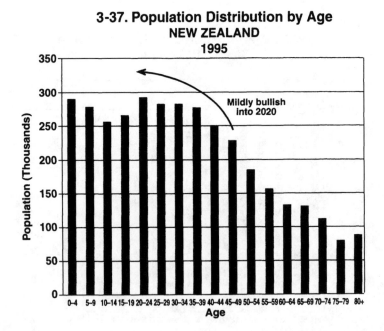

3-37. Population Distribution by Age
NEW ZEALAND
1995

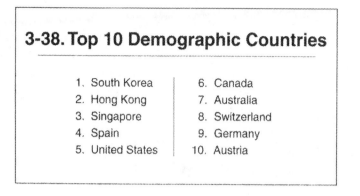

3-38. Top 10 Demographic Countries

1. South Korea   6. Canada
2. Hong Kong   7. Australia
3. Singapore   8. Switzerland
4. Spain   9. Germany
5. United States   10. Austria

rope also very strong but with Japan continuing to lag. The strongest growth will still continue to be in the more-developed Asian countries, despite the recent crisis, with the exception of Japan, which has slowing growth from demographics ahead. I expect Asia to be booming again by 1999 or 2000. The strongest information infrastructures are in North America, northern and western Europe, and the Tiger countries of Asia, as Chart 3-39 (page 110) summarizes.

Chart 3-40 (page 110) shows the countries with the most knowledge-intensive workforces from Nuala Beck in her book *The Next Century*. The surprises here are Singapore as number 2, the Czech Republic as number 9, Switzerland as number 25, and France way down at number 39. This is another important indicator of a country's future potential.

My favorite developed countries overseas for investments are in Asia in the following order: South Korea, Singapore, Hong Kong, and Taiwan. In Europe, I like Spain, Switzerland, Germany, Austria, northern Italy, Great Britain, Norway, and Sweden. In North America, Canada should do almost as well as the United States. And I also like Australia and New Zealand. We can invest in the countries that have the best valuations for the international sector of our portfolios, especially when valuations in the United States are very high. However, I still expect the United States, with the best overall combination of information-technology leadership and strong demographics, to continue to be the best risk/return investment market in the world. The

3-39. Top 20 Information Index Countries

1. Sweden	11. Singapore
2. United States	12. United Kingdom
3. Switzerland	13. Australia
4. Denmark	14. New Zealand
5. Canada	15. Greece
6. France	16. Japan
7. Norway	17. Austria
8. Hong Kong	18. Israel
9. Netherlands	19. Belgium
10. Germany	20. Taiwan

3-40. Top Knowledge-Intensive Workforce Countries*

1. Netherlands	44.1		21. Poland	26.7
2. Singapore	37.3		22. Belgium	—**
3. Germany	37.2		23. Portugal	25.1
4. Denmark	36.7		24. Australia	—
5. New Zealand	36.2		25. Switzerland	19.8
6. United Kingdom	35.9		26. Egypt	17.8 (1995)
7. Sweden	35.6 (1995)		27. Korea	17.0
8. Iceland	35.0		28. Japan	16.1
9. Czech Republic	34.0		29. Venezuela	15.7 (1995)
10. Finland	33.3		30. Mexico	15.5
11. Canada	32.8		31. Malaysia	13.5
12. Norway	32.4		32. Chile	12.0
13. United States	31.9		33. Italy	10.6 (1995)
14. Ireland	31.2		34. Turkey	7.8
15. Israel	30.9		35. Philippines	7.6
16. Hungary	29.4		36. Brazil	7.5 (1995)
17. Austria	28.9 (1995)		37. Thailand	—
18. Hong Kong	28.5		38. Pakistan	6.0 (1995)
19. Spain	27.5		39. France	—
20. Greece	27.0 (1995)			

* Data as of 1996 except where noted.
** A dash (—) indicates that data were not available.
Source: Nuala Beck, *The Next Century* (New York: HarperCollins, 1998), page 14.
Chart data: ILO and Nuala Beck & Associates, Inc.; *Yearbook of Labour Statistics*.

best sectors of Europe should rival or occasionally beat the United States. The greatest overall returns, although with higher risks, should continue to be in the best Asian countries.

Therefore, an understanding of international demographics will represent one of the key advantages for achieving higher returns in a balanced portfolio. In Chapter 4, I will look at the best emerging countries and suggest when to invest in these more volatile markets without taking excessive risks.

CHAPTER 4
International Trends
in Emerging Countries

HERE IS THE PARADOX of investing in emerging countries, from Indonesia to Brazil. Although the greatest demographics of potential spending and growth lie in these countries, age demographics alone are not typically the key driving trend in their economies in the early stages of development. Their populations are concentrated in very low age ranges as a result of very high birth rates and lower life expectancies, and there is a very small middle-class sector due to low technological and skill development. This means that these countries do not tend to follow the consumer-spending and productivity cycles that most developed countries do.

The establishment of stable government structures, free-market systems of commerce, and transportation and communications infrastructures are at first more critical. These countries are like young growing children who need a lot of care and guidance, and the failure of government or "proper parenting" can cause massive problems. That is the reason that investing in these countries is more risky and potentially more rewarding. As we have seen in the crisis in emerging countries in the late 1990s, the failure of government investments and financial systems can cause huge corrections in financial markets even when long-term demographic trends are very favorable. And the demographic trends in developing countries in Asia, Latin America, and Africa are extremely favorable, far more than in North America or Europe.

I recommend investing in emerging countries only for more aggressive investors or in times of extreme undervaluation, as in 1998 in Asia or early 1999 in South America. And only in the countries that have the best demographic, free-market, and infrastructure trends. Only in more-developed countries do you see the legal systems, markets, technological infrastructures, and broad skills and education for consumers and businesses to benefit predictably from fundamental demographic trends. As for the impact of demographics in developing countries, it is more important to see a movement out of the predominance of young age ranges (0–19) into the more productive and higher spending twenties, thirties, and forties. High birth and high mortality rates are a formula for a sustained poverty cycle—too many unproductive kids and too few productive adults.

Paradoxically, in emerging countries you want to see falling birth rates, but simultaneously increasing life expectancies and increasing proportions of the population moving into middle-class living standards. The first sign of that will tend to be the formation of a generation bulge in the late teens to twenties, as is occurring in countries like Thailand, Brazil, and Mexico. And since politics are more critical, you want to see prudent investments in infrastructures, freer markets, and movements toward more democratic government and legal systems, as well as stable currencies and capital flows into the country.

To summarize, third world countries start with steeply downward-sloping age distributions with very high numbers of young people and lower numbers of more productive older people, as in Kenya or India. Then as a third world country starts to industrialize successfully, you see the beginnings of generation bulges, usually in the teens or twenties. As a country becomes more developed, distinct generation bulges tend to form into the twenties, thirties, and forties, ultimately as in the United States or Germany. And finally, the most mature cultures, as in France or New Zealand, which have low birth rates and low rates of innovation and change, tend to move toward flatter overall age distributions and generation bulges. You also want to see expanding information infrastructures, from phones and cell phones to TVs and PCs. I will therefore refer to the *Wired* information index I used in Chapter 3 for developed countries. These indexes will not be as high as in developed countries. It is the relative rating to other emerging countries that will be critical to compare. The higher ranges would fall between 8 and 13 in emerging countries.

The Emerging Countries in Asia

Let's start with my favorite international region. Asia has the strongest age demographics and strong growth trends in information infrastructure development in the emerging third world. And countries from Indonesia to Thailand saw the strongest corrections and the best values in stock prices back in 1998.

China (Chart 4-1) has the strongest overall demographic picture, with a 1.2 billion population that is rapidly moving from rural to urban areas, as occurred in the United States from the late 1800s into the 1900s. This is occurring despite government restrictions on births,

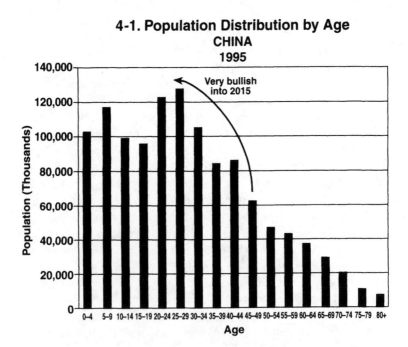

4-1. Population Distribution by Age
CHINA
1995

which is again a good sign for developing countries. China has formed two generation bulges, one peaking at age 25–29 in 1995 and the other at age 5–9. This is an important sign that a country is transitioning from a third world to an industrializing nation successfully, as mentioned at the beginning of this chapter. China's economy should have very strong overall demographic spending and productivity trends into around 2015 to 2020 before a 5- to 10-year downturn in spending. But China's growth may be a bit slower from around 2000 to 2005 because of a small dip in demographics in that time period.

Like Japan and the rest of Asia, China has a large debt overhang from subsidizing public and favored industries. Therefore, it is not my most-favored country in the coming years but should be one of the very strongest from 2005 into 2015 to 2020. This makes it a good investment play for equities when the United States and many developed countries see declining economies and stock markets after 2009 or so. On the information index, China rates a moderately healthy 8 for an emerging country. But its rate of growth in infrastructure development is very strong as more people move from rural to urban areas at the fastest rate in the world.

Of the younger more-emerging countries in Asia outside China, only Thailand has developed a large generation bulge beyond the youngest years (Chart 4-2, page 116). You can see a bulge occurring from age 15–19 into 25–29. That is a very good sign of industrialization and middle-class development. Thailand's boom should be very strong and last until around 2025 before an extended downturn due to demographic factors. Most important, Thailand rates a very healthy 10 on the information index. It was the first emerging country to attract strong foreign investment and capital flows after the severe crisis of 1997 and 1998. This country is also a very popular resort and vacation destination. Its one drawback may be the minor devastation being caused by the AIDS epidemic on its population demographics.

Indonesia, Malaysia, and the Philippines are still countries largely in the emerging or third world stage, with very young populations predominating and steep declines in older, more productive age ranges. Indonesia (Chart 4-3, page 116) seems to be emerging out of a third world pattern most rapidly, with a slight relative generation bulge into the ages of 20–24, perhaps because of its strong tourism industries. But Indonesia's strongest disadvantage is that it rates only a 7 on

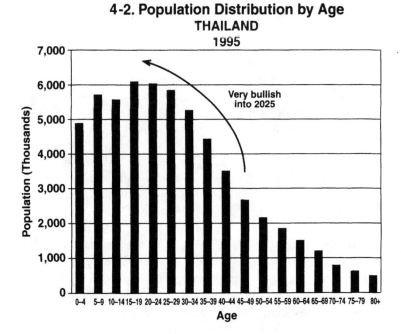

4-2. Population Distribution by Age
THAILAND
1995

Very bullish
into 2025

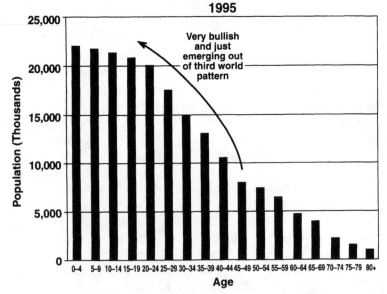

4-3. Population Distribution by Age
INDONESIA
1995

Very bullish
and just
emerging out
of third world
pattern

the information index. The country has so many diverse cultures and dialects over many islands that, like Africa, it is hard to unite into a strong industrial- and information-driven economy.

Malaysia (Chart 4-4) has an odd pattern of fewer people in the 15–19 and 20–24 age ranges, perhaps due to very high birth rates in rural areas despite the growth in urban areas like Kuala Lumpur. But here's the kicker and why I still like Malaysia: It rates a whopping 13 on the information index because of the rapid development of high-tech infrastructures in Kuala Lumpur. Malaysia may be the best investment buy in Asia as their political and financial structures are forced to evolve toward more free-market and democratic structures. But that is a necessary ingredient, and the political leadership has been very questionable since the Asian crisis hit in late 1997. Malaysia seems to be a very mixed country with extreme urban development and a very third world agricultural economy in its rural regions. But expect Kuala Lumpur to continue to be a magnet for migration and growth in the coming decade in this relatively small geographical re-

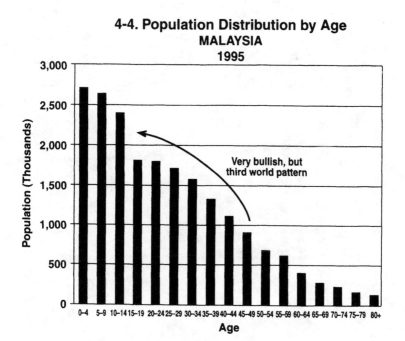

4-4. Population Distribution by Age
MALAYSIA
1995

Very bullish, but third world pattern

gion. I would recommend investing here on further political or finan cial setbacks, as the fundamentals of growth are too strong for the government to mess it up for long.

In the Philippines (Chart 4-5), note the very steeply declining age distribution from young to old that is characteristic of third world countries. The Philippines has survived the crisis of 1998 the best of all the emerging countries in Asia. That says something for their government and political structures. It bodes well for prosperity in the coming decade. Indonesia and Malaysia still have many political uncertainties, with Malaysia looking a bit better than Indonesia coming out of the recent crisis. I would invest in these countries only if I saw major changes toward free-market financial and political systems. Although that may be inevitable, it has yet to be seen. For now, the Philippines may be the best bet, with Malaysia a close second. Indonesia holds the greatest potential for growth if political trends reverse in the right direction. Vietnam is also an up-and-coming country showing positive signs of development and growth.

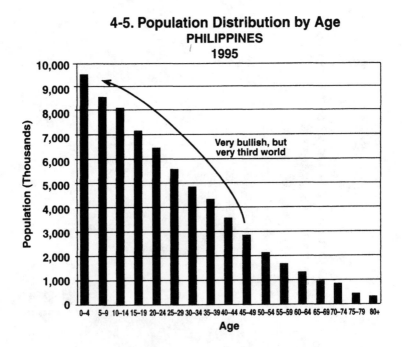

4-5. Population Distribution by Age
PHILIPPINES
1995

To summarize, trends for developing countries in Asia look very strong for the coming decade, despite the weakness that is likely to continue in Japan. Paradoxically, the economic crises that have occurred in the emerging countries of Asia have tended only to accelerate the movement toward freer markets and more democratic governments. I think we will look back in a decade and see that the crisis in Asia was the best thing that ever happened to that region. And I think that the emerging countries in Asia will grow and prosper at the highest rates in the world. But I want to see the political and financial trends change. Until then I am more than happy to invest in the more-developed countries that have strong potential, including South Korea, Hong Kong, Singapore, and Taiwan.

If governments and financial systems are overhauled, the emerging countries, from Thailand to the Philippines to Malaysia to Indonesia, should prove to be very lucrative investments. I prefer to buy them only in deep crises like that of 1998 or on strong pullbacks in the future. That way you can minimize your downside risk in these volatile markets. Otherwise, we can benefit from the growth of these emerging countries by investing in the leading multinational companies, as was covered in Chapter 2.

Latin America, the Most Developed of Emerging Regions

Latin America, from Central to South America and the Caribbean, also holds great potential for investment profits in the coming decade. The movement from rural to urban areas is more advanced, and hence the information infrastructures are as well. But the overall demographics, skills, and infrastructures have less growth potential than in Asia. Latin America is therefore a slightly less risky investment in the emerging-country arena, with good long-term returns. But there has been and still will be more volatility than in developed markets like North America and Europe.

Let's start with Mexico, the country most tied to the fortunes of the strongest developed region in the world, North America. That is Mexico's greatest strength. Not only does this country have the most advantageous location for exporting manufactured and agricultural goods to the United States and Canada, but we are here to bail

Mexico out when it has financial problems, as in 1995, Why? Because our economy and our ethnic demographics are more dependent on Mexico.

Mexico (Chart 4-6) has the more classic third world chart, much like that of Indonesia. It is showing the bare beginnings of a generation bulge into the 15–19 and 20–24 age cohorts. With the successful transition to the Free Trade Zone in North America (NAFTA), Mexico stands to benefit from growing trade with the United States and Canada in commodity products and components because of its lower wage rates and proximity. Mexico's younger age distribution also provides a balance to the aging populations in North America. In fact, Mexico's chart looks slightly more advanced toward development than Indonesia's. Therefore, I am very bullish on Mexico for the coming decade and beyond. And Mexico rates a very strong 11 for an emerging country on the information index, well ahead of the emerging countries in Asia.

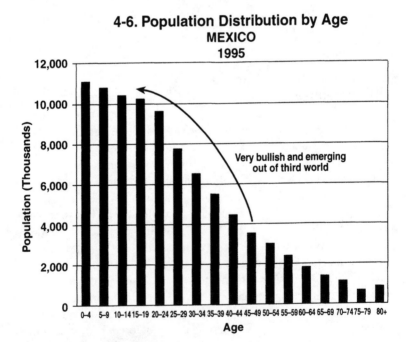

4-6. Population Distribution by Age
MEXICO
1995

For the most-developed emerging countries, you have to look to the more temperate areas of South America, like Chile and Argentina, where urban migration has been the greatest and where the information index ranks a very strong 13 for both countries. More temperate and colder climates have tended to encourage higher degrees of technological advancement throughout history because of the challenges of living in and migrating to such climates. As in Australia and New Zealand, this seems to be true in the most southern or cooler levels of South America. In warmer and more tropical zones, people seem to be more comfortable and happy, which is not as conducive to innovation. But air-conditioning since the mid-1900s seems to be changing that!

In Chile (Chart 4-7) you can see that there is a very definite generation bulge developing between the ages of 15 and 34. That is a very good sign of emergence into industrialization and a middle-class economy. Chile looks to be the most-developed country in South and Latin

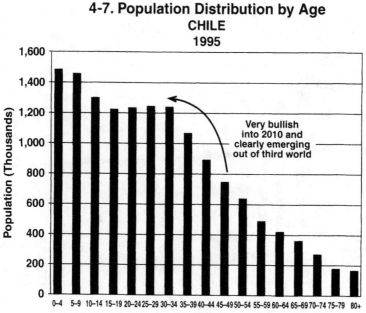

4-7. Population Distribution by Age
CHILE
1995

Very bullish
into 2010 and
clearly emerging
out of third world

America. The demographic trends are very bullish into around 2010 and then relatively flat or buoyant into 2025 before growth should resume strongly again. Therefore, Chile represents my highest recommendation for investment, along with Mexico because of its proximity to the booming region of North America.

Argentina (Chart 4-8) is the next-most-developed country in South America. It has a strong information index of 13, as Chile does, and a distinct generation bulge forming in the 15–19 age cohort. But the demographic trends here are not as strong as in Chile. We should see moderate growth into 2015 and then stronger growth into 2025. Both Chile and Argentina should represent strong investments for our portfolios after the boom peaks in the United States in 2009.

Brazil (Chart 4-9) demonstrates an economy transitioning toward industrialization but still having more third world characteristics. It has the greatest population concentration for South America

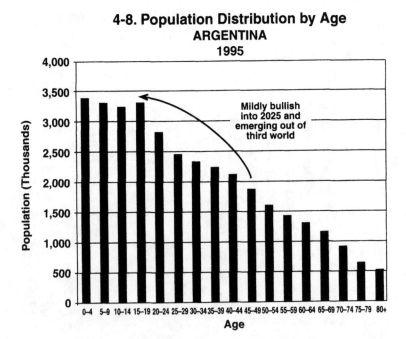

4-8. Population Distribution by Age
ARGENTINA
1995

Mildly bullish into 2025 and emerging out of third world

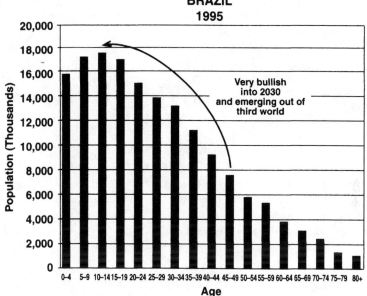

4-9. Population Distribution by Age
BRAZIL
1995

Very bullish
into 2030
and emerging out of
third world

and the Western Hemisphere, and it is showing signs of emerging successfully, despite the series of financial crises in 1998 and early 1999. Births are declining, and a generation bulge is developing in the 10–14 range as of 1995. Therefore, Brazil is not a country to be ignored. Demographic trends should be very favorable all the way out to 2030 if the country can maintain a stable political structure. Although Brazil obviously would not be expected to rate as high as Chile and Argentina on the information index, it scores a very respectable 11, right along with Mexico. This will be another country to focus on in the next downturn in the United States and should rebound very strongly from the 60% to 70% correction in 1998 and early 1999.

I am not going to focus on the age demographics of the rest of Central and South America, but the growth rates throughout should be strong as a general rule. Not only are population growth and demographics very positive, but information infrastructures are very strong, thanks to tourism and proximity to the United States. Bermuda has a very wealthy population and rates a 20 on the information index, as does the Cayman Islands. Many of the Caribbean islands, from Puerto Rico to Barbados, have information indexes as high as 16 or 17. Even Jamaica and Costa Rica rate 12 on the information index. The Dominican Republic rates an 11. The countries in Central and northern South America rate in the ranges of 10 for Ecuador to 9 for El Salvador, Guyana, and Peru to 8 for Bolivia, Honduras, and Paraguay to 7 for Cuba and Guatemala. The lowest rating is for Haiti at 6. And of course, there we see the highest poverty rates.

These ratings are much higher in general than for most African countries and for many less-developed countries in the Far East simply because of proximity to the United States. Therefore, Latin America looks bullish overall for investors who can take higher risks in the coming decade. And many countries, such as Chile, Argentina, and Brazil, look good even in the next downturn after 2009. My strongest recommendations for investing would include Chile, Mexico, and Argentina in Central and South America, and in the Caribbean, Barbados and Puerto Rico (because of its strong connection with the United States). Resort areas in the Caribbean, especially the more upscale, also warrant consideration because of the strong vacation and leisure cycle for baby boomers in North America in the coming decade and beyond.

The Emerging Countries in the Middle East

The Middle East, from Israel to Saudi Arabia, represents a unique region because of its volatile political nature as well as the dominance of oil in that region. These risky factors keep the Middle East from being one of my favorite regions for investment.

Israel is the most interesting and perhaps the most attractive of the countries here. It ranks a very strong 18 on the information index and in many ways is more like a developed country. But it has an age distribution (Chart 4-10) more like that of an emerging country. This indicates a very mixed economic culture with high urbanization in one sector of the economy and, in another sector, strong rural populations with high birth rates. The demographics suggest only mild

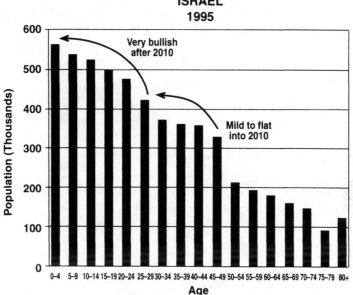

4-10. Population Distribution by Age
ISRAEL
1995

growth into around 2010, then very high growth rates for decades to follow. The strong information structures and high-knowledge-based industries would suggest Israel should grow faster than its demographics. Therefore, this country should represent good investment potential into the next decade and perhaps very great potential in the next downturn after 2009. But of course, the volatile nature of the social and political systems in the region brings substantial risks.

Despite the growth in the world, especially in emerging nations with high populations, oil prices have been fluctuating within a pretty narrow range outside the Iraqi crisis in 1990. I don't expect oil prices to rise much in the coming decade because of expanding technologies and the discovery of new oil reserves around the developing world. Since oil is the driving factor for exports in this region, I expect economic growth overall to be slower than in the rest of the world. Demographics in major countries like Saudi Arabia would support that projection.

Saudi Arabia (Chart 4-11) has a peak in the 35–39 age cohort as of 1995, meaning that growth should be modest into around 2005 and then down modestly into 2015. But then this country could see explosive growth after 2015 if the political scene remains stable. Therefore, I would not expect strong growth in the Middle East in the coming decade and even decline after 2005. I would definitely place my bets on Israel if I had to, but this is not a favored region for investing overall in the worldwide boom.

The Emerging Countries in Africa

Many people ask me why Africa has remained so undeveloped over the centuries, despite being the cradle of civilization. I would have to defer the answer to Thomas Sowell, an African American

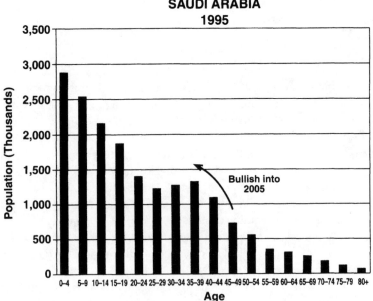

4-11. Population Distribution by Age
SAUDI ARABIA
1995

scholar who is a fellow at the Hoover Institute and a columnist for *Forbes*. He attributes the slow evolution in Africa largely to geography. And his argument makes a lot of sense. Evolution depends on communication and the spread of new ideas, technology, and knowledge. That is why information and technology revolutions have been so critical in history. It is also why isolated island cultures have typically developed so slowly over history. Sowell notes that Africa has a very unique geography that limits communications, making it more like a large island overall and internally like a lot of small island cultures.

First, most of the river systems are not continuous, as in the United States, Europe, Latin America, and Asia. There are abrupt waterfalls, as well as times of year when many rivers dry up altogether. The Nile is the only exception. This has kept trade and communications over rivers minimal. The Industrial Revolution was first manifested through steamships and river travel in Europe and North America. The greatest part of northern Africa contains the largest and harshest desert in the world, also making travel, trade, and communications extremely difficult. Even in the coastal regions there are almost no natural harbors, making Africa less accessible for trade and communications by sea.

These geographical limitations have kept Africa largely isolated from the rest of the world, and villages and cultures stay largely isolated within. As a result, Africa is composed of many cultures and dialects. And information infrastructures are the least developed of any continent in the world. The paradox and challenge of the coming era is that Africa could benefit the most, relatively speaking, from the expansion of the global Internet, especially through satellite and wireless technologies, but Africa has the lowest penetration of such information infrastructures. The broad variety of cultures and dialects would make Internet-based communication more difficult.

In addition to stabilization of political and financial systems, the most important factor for Africa will be investments in information systems that can unite, educate, and standardize the language and communications customs of its people. I would want to see progress in those areas before investing in African countries as a general rule. South Africa should be the bellwether country for measuring whether such progress is being made effectively.

South Africa boasts the most modern African city, Cape Town. It is showing modest signs of growth and development, but it still has a long way to go. There is still very strong inequality of incomes, which shows the lack of development of a substantial middle-class sector and can lead to social and political unrest. Chart 4-12 shows that even South Africa still has the age distribution pattern of a third world country. Its information index at 11 is strong for Africa but still very weak compared to Latin America. The demographic trends are bullish if the political and social systems continue to evolve.

Egypt (Chart 4-13) shows slightly more signs of developing, with slight generation bulges at ages 35–44 and 5–9. The information index here of 9, though modest, is in the upper ranges for Africa. Egypt may just be emerging from a third world pattern, as may Kenya (Chart 4-14), which has an information index of only 5, but these countries are still largely undeveloped. Morocco actually looks the most promis-

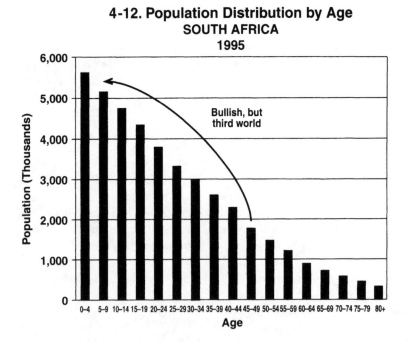

4-12. Population Distribution by Age
SOUTH AFRICA
1995

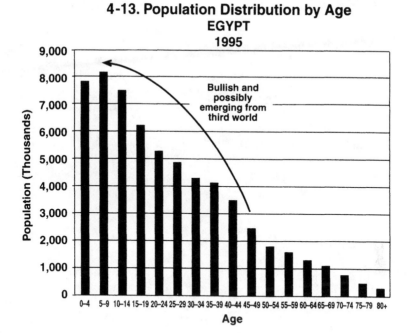

4-13. Population Distribution by Age
EGYPT
1995

Population (Thousands)

Bullish and
possibly
emerging from
third world

Age

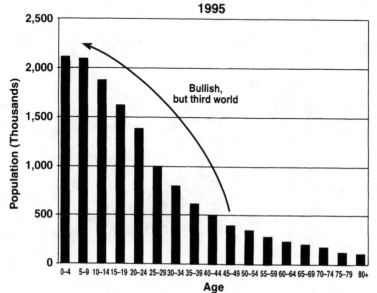

4-14. Population Distribution by Age
KENYA
1995

Population (Thousands)

Bullish,
but third world

Age

ing from the demographics point of view. In Chart 4-15 we can see a generation bulge starting to form in the 10–19 age range. And its information index rates a pretty healthy 8. Because of their proximity to Europe, I would expect that North African countries like Egypt and Morocco to be the best bets. But overall, I don't recommend Africa as an investment option for most investors, the biggest reason being that the information infrastructures rate extremely low for most countries. The extremes include ratings of only 1 for Somalia, Niger, Liberia, Chad, and Congo. Development simply can't occur to any significant degree without the capacities for communication and learning.

The Outlook for India

Despite a burgeoning middle-class sector in the minority, India (Chart 4-16) overall still has more of a third world chart and is not

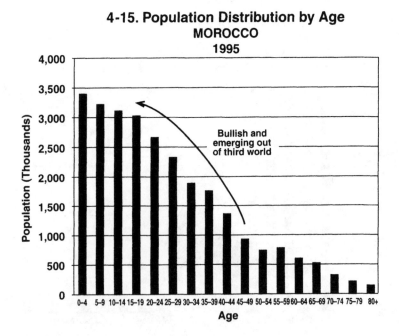

4-15. Population Distribution by Age
MOROCCO
1995

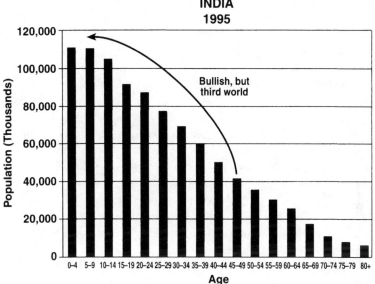

**4-16. Population Distribution by Age
INDIA
1995**

likely to see as strong or steady growth and expansion as China in the coming decades. India is very much two countries in one. It has strong middle-class sectors and a growing high-tech industry. But it is still largely a third world country, as you can see in Chart 4-16. India's stock markets also tend to have a volatile pattern that suggests unstable politics. And its information index rates a mere 6. Therefore, I generally favor emerging countries in Asia over India for most investors.

Summary of Investment Recommendations

Emerging-country investments are generally too volatile and risky for most investors. The best way to play the massive growth of the industrialization of the third world is through large multinational companies in the United States, Europe, and Japan. I personally prefer investing in emerging countries only when the markets have seen extreme corrections (as in late 1997 to early 1999). By investing at the lowest valuations, you can minimize the downside risk and participate in the strong long-term growth of these countries. Asia was the great opportunity in late 1997 and late 1998, as was Latin America in early 1999. Asia both has the strongest demographics in the decades ahead and took the greatest correction. The second rule is to diversify if you are investing in emerging-country funds. Don't bet on one country or region.

In Part 3, I will focus on perhaps the most important consideration: how to take the bigger picture and use financial planning to achieve your highest goals. Money is ultimately about creating the freedom to live the lifestyle you want. Hence, you should start with formulating your highest goals and then consider how your investment strategies can help you achieve those goals and aspirations. Let's get out of the financial realm and move to where the rubber meets the road. What do you want to do with the rest of your life? Or "to be or not to be . . . that is the question"!

What do you want to be? I'll start in Chapter 5 with a new view of retirement and why you should consider creating a new, more fulfilling lifestyle well before you retire.

PART 3

Planning a Great Life After the Boom

CHAPTER 5
Don't Retire . . .
Live Life Fully
and Make a Difference

BABY BOOMERS are just starting to think about retirement en masse as they move into their forties and fifties. One thing is for sure. This generation will change retirement, just as they have changed every stage of life they have entered. So it's time to start thinking differently about your lifestyle and your retirement, whatever your age. The prosperity of the coming decade and new communications technologies are going to make new lifestyles possible well before and into your retirement.

In Chart 5-1 (page 136) we can see that our life expectancies have made tremendous gains over the last century, more than at any other time in history. This has contributed greatly to our economic growth and prosperity, because people who live longer learn more, earn more, spend more, and contribute more. The average life expectancy is estimated to have been around age 22 to 25 for most of biblical times forward. It started rising in the 1700s, moving toward 35 by 1800, and then to around 47 by 1900. Then in just one century it advanced 30 years! But note that the greatest acceleration came between the 1890s and 1940s, when the gains averaged about 4 years every decade. Since then it has slowed to more like 1.5 years per decade.

However, the coming wave of genetic technologies is likely to cause another wave of faster expansion sometime early in the next cen-

5-1. Life Expectancy at Birth

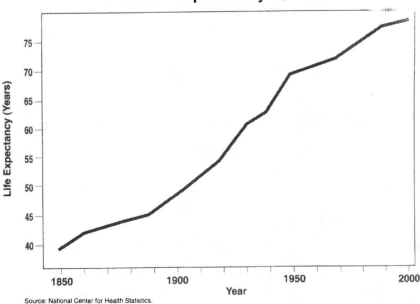

Source: National Center for Health Statistics.

tury. My best estimate is that this could occur from around the 2010s into the 2060s and that our life expectancies could advance toward 110 to 120. Throughout history that has been the maximum age that the healthiest and luckiest people have lived.

The clear insight is this: You should plan to live longer than your parents. Do you think they expected to live so long when they were your age? Although the average life expectancy is 77 today, for a male who has reached the age of 65 it is 80. For a female it is 84. But let's say you are 40 today; four decades from now, when you are 80, that life expectancy is likely to have moved up to 86 for males and 90 for females. It is very likely that we will see an acceleration in life expectancy gains by then that would push your life expectancy several more years out. Hence, you should plan for the likelihood of living into your late eighties at the minimum or into your nineties and possibly beyond. The younger you are today, the longer you should plan to live.

That brings up the obvious question: If you thought you would live into your nineties, would you totally drop out, retire at age 65, and just play golf or shuffleboard in Miami? We aren't just living longer, but the quality of our life and health into older age ranges has been improving dramatically. The new retirement ethic will be this simple. Retirement will be redefined as a time of freedom when you can do what you really want, what is most meaningful to you, after you are freed of your obligations for career and child rearing. And this will be a very long stage of life for most of us. But let's go another step and suggest that this period of freedom to pursue your highest lifestyle and goals should more naturally start in your late forties to early fifties or when your kids leave the nest, not in your sixties.

That is the purpose of the midlife crisis. To reconsider what you are going to do the rest of your life once you have reached the pinnacle of your career and family cycle. You should change the direction of your life, possibly even radically. We should welcome and leverage this natural period of transition instead of fighting it, as most people do. The best way to do that is to start meeting with a therapist, counselor, mentor, or support group and begin to ask yourself some very basic questions. Why wait until you are 65 or 70 to move to your definition of paradise, whether it be an island or a golf resort or a desert hilltop or a beach or a ski slope or even right downtown where there is the greatest access to dining, arts, and sports? Why wait until you are 65 or 70 to take some time off and focus on what you would most like to accomplish or contribute to society? Why not start doing that now or in your late forties or early fifties? Why not start planning for this event before it occurs, in your late twenties or thirties? Or maybe you haven't fully gone through that midlife crisis, even if you are well into your fifties or sixties.

> **The most important dimension of your financial plan should not be merely how you can survive through retirement but how you can create the lifestyle and life work you most desire well before the typical retirement age, if possible. Such freedom comes from the security of being able to live off your financial investments.**

I am suggesting that should be your goal for the next decade or so, to become financially independent as shortly after your kids leave the nest as possible. That certainly doesn't mean you should plan to drop out and not work. I think most of us are going to choose to work full-time, part-time, or for charitable causes, but in arenas of our choosing. Having sufficient assets to cover your basic living costs from your investments or at least from minimal earnings gives you that full freedom, even if you plan to continue to work well into retirement and expand your spending power and financial resources. If you don't need the financial resources to live off fully, they still enhance your capacity to start your own business, help out your kids or grandkids, or contribute more meaningfully to causes that you value.

This urge to pursue your highest goals, to determine your own destiny, to contribute the most you have to society and others has been termed "self-actualization" by psychologists. It is generally considered to be the highest stage of human development outside more esoteric spiritual stages of development. Abraham Maslow was the most noted in developing a very clear and simple hierarchy of human needs, as we can see in Chart 5-2, which I am reprinting from Chapter 9 in *The Roaring 2000s*.

Our needs rise from survival to belonging to self-esteem to self-actualization. Many psychologists have broken these stages into many substages, but this is a very valid model that is similar to and largely consistent with most psychological models of human development. The freedom to move into a lifestyle of self-actualization comes only from the positive self-image, skills, success, and resources that tend to emerge from the self-esteem stage. That is why it makes sense to achieve strong goals and build financial success and not feel guilty about it. It is a natural and useful stage in human evolution. And that capacity comes only from the ability first to meet your most basic survival needs and then to learn to fit into the needs of your community or society by learning to follow the rules that lead to effective functioning within that group.

It is in the self-esteem stage that we develop the ability to set goals and achieve them and to develop systems and plans for achieving those goals. Instead of obeying the rules, we learn to set them. We learn to think for ourselves, make our own decisions, and appreciate different ways for achieving our goals. We learn to appreciate the different talents of others and how we can work with them. We learn to meet our own needs for growth and development so that we can optimize our ability to function and create the living circumstance that fits our most desired lifestyle.

5-2. Maslow's Hierarchy of Human Needs

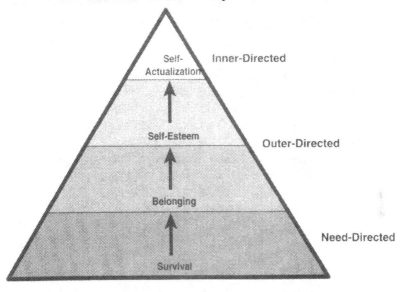

We develop the ability to learn from our experience and change our life strategies to better meet our goals. To summarize, we become effective. We start to take charge of our own destiny. We no longer have to follow the direction of others childishly by merely following the rules. We can begin to create our own destiny. Most important, we meet our material needs for comfort and self-expression. We find our niche in life and our means for success. But that is only the prelude for the higher stage of self-actualization.

The stage of self-actualization emerges when we start to care less about our own material achievements. We care about what has the most meaning for us in life, what creates the most satisfaction for us personally—whether that be sharing more time with family and friends or contributing more to society and our community or changing the world or whatever. Our horizon expands.

The real trend in human evolution is that we become less egocentric as we evolve, just as kids do as they grow up. We move from survival and security, meeting our most basic needs; to belonging, to a group, fitting in and following the rules of that group; to achieving success and self-esteem on our own merits and goals, which meets our highest material needs; to finding our own unique role in the greater society, which meets both our highest needs for meaning and our greatest contribution to society—on our own terms.

We learn to combine an appreciation of what we do best, how we want to work and live, and how that can uniquely contribute to society and the greater good. Think about it this way. If all people did what they did best and found the best way to contribute their talents to society with a minimum of expensive and bureaucratic government and corporate direction, wouldn't we have a much more productive and humane society? Wouldn't that represent a self-managing network capable of great effectiveness and great change?

So once we start to meet our needs for achievement and self-esteem, it is time to start considering what has the most meaning for us in life and how that could most contribute to society at large. This is truly the best of all worlds for both the individual lifestyle and the good of our greater culture. It has been thought in the past that the best way for people to contribute to society is to sacrifice their needs and lifestyle for the good of the family, community, and society. As more of us become capable of evaluating our own strengths and weaknesses and charting our own goals and destinies, we can create greater contributions to society by doing what we do best, and achieve greater meaning by finding ways to benefit others. We become not just achievers, but leaders in our own realms, champions of our own causes.

Much has been communicated about self-esteem and self-actualization and creating your own lifestyle and destiny by such motivators as Abraham Maslow, Anthony Robbins, and Stephen Covey. But the truth for most of us is that the demands of our career and family have very likely compromised that freedom, even if we have already made great strides toward success and self-esteem. It is appropriate to provide for your family and for your needs in your career cycle. It is appropriate to achieve the lifestyle that you need to meet those needs. It is appropriate to develop your skills and financial resources first by contributing your skills to society in the way that it demands and rewards. That is the essence of the self-esteem stage. But the real opportunity to flower and meet your highest human needs comes after you

have achieved those needs and have the capacity to choose what you
really want to do.

We should see the period from our midlife crisis, on or after
the kids leave the nest, as the greatest opportunity for pursuing
our most cherished goals and for creating a lifestyle with no
compromises that contributes the most to society.

Jim Collins, bestselling author of *Built to Last*, has a great way of
bringing this issue into reality. "What would you do if you had ten
years to live and $10 million in the bank?" That is a great question to
ask now, even if you don't have the $10 million or think you have
much longer than that to live. It allows you to start to get a vision of
where you would like to be in 10 years, at the top of this boom, or
shortly after, when your kids leave the nest. Or more immediately if
you do happen to have the financial resources now.

Please note that I am not recommending the path of severe aus-
terity to reach financial security, as was touted in *The Millionaire Next
Door*. To build up financial resources that you never spend and create
only out of fear of the worst that could happen is more suggestive of
the security and survival stage of Maslow's hierarchy of needs. In an
era of incredible opportunities for specialization in skills and contributions to society, to spend all your time mowing your own lawn, trim-
ming your own trees, clipping coupons to save a few cents here and
there does not represent a lifestyle that many of us would cherish. I
consider that penny-wise and pound-foolish. Would we have wanted
Bill Gates and Mother Teresa to waste their valuable time mowing
their own lawns? Didn't they best contribute by focusing on what they
do best and their own vision of the future? Why shouldn't we look at
our own lives from this perspective?

The baby boom generation is the first generation of dual-income
families who have even less time for stressful, uptight approaches to
life. Isn't there a better way to grow and contribute to our culture? Are
you supposed to die rich after never having enjoyed your life or financial resources? What . . . and hand it all to the kids so they can go to
Palm Beach and party for the rest of their lives? Does this really make
sense to you? Wouldn't it make more sense to hand your kids and
grandkids enough money to provide for their education and entrepre-

neural needs and then donate the rest to meaningful causes in society? Is merely accumulating money your highest goal in life? How many people have you seen with that primary goal who are truly happy? Cutting back to the simple life and driving an old car and living in a smaller house has been recommended in many books as a way to both simplify your life and create less need for income so that you can have more time for basic relationships. That certainly could make sense up to a point. But what can you really do from such a poor position? Will you really contribute more to society just by conserving some basic resources? Does this represent a higher quality of life for a new era or a retrenchment back to the past, a reaction to today's changes and challenges? The reality of history is that today's challenges greatly raise the quality of our lives and our standard of living if we embrace them instead of retreating from them. In *The Roaring 2000s*, I give a more detailed account of what life was like at the turn of the last century and why the "good old days" weren't nearly as good as we nostalgically assume.

For some people the values of simplicity and basic living are paramount and represent the optimal choice and the lifestyle they desire. That is totally appropriate. We should all have the freedom to choose. But the rest of us shouldn't be pushed into a guilt trip for desiring to push the envelope on human evolution and move forward. And that doesn't mean wasting money or spending everything we make, living for today only and not saving for the future or contributing to society. It just means we don't have to take such a restrictive view of our lifestyles and the role of money in our lives. Money should represent freedom and expanded energy for life, not a restriction on life. *The Millionaire Next Door* was a great revelation about the real lives of many wealthy people. But it should be seen as a lesson in how *not* to create a self-actualized lifestyle.

In Chapters 1 and 2, I showed how, for the first time in history, we can see economic trends over the rest of our lifetime and how we can position our portfolios to prosper in good and bad times. Therefore, I am suggesting that you don't have to scrimp and save every penny you can for the next great depression, even though such an economic environment will very likely occur to some degree after 2009. As I will show in the next chapter, such times bring beneficial trends for the people who have the financial power to survive and prosper. There will be many more sectors of our society that will need our skills and contributions. New opportunities and new needs will emerge rapidly. Prices and the cost of living actually fall in such times. This is another reason you don't need to be so paranoid about the costs of retirement if you are systematically building your wealth today.

In difficult periods like the 1930s or 1970s, business opportunities and innovations thrive for those who have the freedom to see change as opportunity instead of threat. This is when new products and industries begin to emerge. In fact, the real truth about wealth is that it is easier to build in bad times than in good. But you have to see those downturns coming and not be overwhelmed by the difficult trends. Most people are caught in jobs or businesses or lifestyles or equity investments or real estate that quickly become obsolete or devalued. Few have the attention in such a struggle to see the new trends and take advantage of them. What is difficult in deflationary periods like the 1930s and 2010s ahead is that work is hard to find and old businesses are hard to sustain. But if you have a secure career, or better, have created your own business or nonprofit institution by then, or have built the financial assets in this incredible boom to have financial security, your living costs will be lower, your business and contribution opportunities will actually expand, and your freedom to enjoy life will be greater.

The real question to start asking yourself now is: What do I really want to do with the rest of my life?

Is there a business you would like to start, or would you rather create a part-time job with your company and have more time to pursue hobbies or charitable pursuits? Or is there a cause or charity that you would like to support more intensely with donations or personal time and energy? You can create a charitable trust, with strong tax advantages, that pays you a fixed income and transfers your assets to that charity when you die. Or you could create your own nonprofit charity. There are tax incentives that could help make that a reality faster than you think. I will look more at those tax benefits and options in Chapter 8. But you should be asking these questions first to determine what goals and visions you have for the coming decades.

Where would you live if you could live anywhere? Maybe that is halfway around the world. Maybe with the tax savings of some states or countries, you could pay for or rent a vacation home where you live now and live in a new, exotic place, creating the best of both worlds. One of the paradigm shifts I covered in *The Roaring 2000s* is that more people are going to choose to live in attractive smaller towns and communities, from resort areas to college towns to exurbs outside major cities. I gave many types of boomtowns to consider and many examples of emerging boomtowns, like DeWees Island, South Carolina; McCall, Idaho; and Carbondale, Colorado.

The new paradigm shift becomes most extreme when you realize that you could live in a resort area and have your vacation home in the downtown of a major city. Talk about the best of both worlds! This is possible for many in this era only because of radical advances in transportation and communication technologies. You may find that you are much more effective when you can alternate between a highly active lifestyle in an urban area and a more creative lifestyle in an attractive recreational area.

The real key to self-actualization lies in first understanding your unique needs and talents. What do you need to grow and learn? What can you best contribute to others with your talents? What have you learned or experienced in life that is unique? How does that allow you to create a personal vision of what could be better in this world? What new products or services are needed for people like you? What deserving causes and needs aren't being met that you could serve? What injustices that you are most familiar with need to be addressed? And how would your unique experiences, insights, and skills serve those causes?

Once you develop such a vision of how you could contribute, then comes the reality of what it will take to make that vision a reality. What people or skills could augment your vision and how could you network with them? What resources or funding would you need? What technology and systems would be required to make this happen?

The truth is that the great creative, visionary, and effective leaders and entrepreneurs at the greatest and the most everyday levels are people who understand the simple secret to the creative process. It starts with a compelling vision, something you intuitively know is possible even if it doesn't presently exist. It is the strength of that vision that drives the process, not excessive planning and goal setting. Such a strong vision of change creates an unavoidable tension between the present reality and your compelling vision that it forces a resolution toward the vision. The fact that this compelling vision is not reality becomes unacceptable. That motivates you and the people you enlist to accomplish your vision to confront and deal with those unacceptable realities until the vision manifests itself.

How that happens cannot be totally planned. Such a vision naturally sets up a process that forces you to "go with the flow." This is something that most great people, from sports figures to business entrepreneurs to political leaders, directly experience and can describe to us. You become so totally absorbed in the process or vision that you become it! Your responses and actions come naturally. Challenges and difficulties present themselves when needed, and hence you confront them. That doesn't mean that the process is easy. It is difficult, but the vision makes it worthwhile. Solutions come when least expected, often from unexpected sources and insights. Your plans quickly change to new ones. Your failures become your greatest path to success.

It's not that you don't plan and set goals at each stage, but that they quickly become obsolete as your direct and intuitive experience brings new insights and new opportunities that a strict planning and goal-setting process would not have foreseen or taken into account. Then you set new goals and plans based on those insights, and new insights and goals come from those, and so on.

A strong vision and purpose creates a dynamic process that is flowing and defies bureaucracy and control. It creates a "path of least resistance," like a river flowing to its source through the best path possible, constantly changing course as necessary. This creates the best way to "get there," even if that doesn't seem to be the case as you are going down the cascades. Only in retrospect do you realize that it was the best path.

Wouldn't that be the best way to achieve your life goals? Wouldn't that be the best way to help your kids achieve their goals? They have a higher level of self-esteem and self-actualization than we did as kids. Hence, we need to learn to guide them differently as well.

Helping Your Kids Achieve Self-Esteem . . . and Self-Actualization

Do you want to help your kids start their own business or create a charitable institution of their own or become involved in your charitable cause instead of just taking on a normal job? Many small business owners dream of passing their business to their kids, which may be great for the kids. But it may not be. Don't force your kids to live your dreams, as many of our parents tried to do. Our jobs are far more exciting than our parents' jobs were and have increasingly combined fun with work, self-esteem, and self-actualization instead of just surviving and belonging. Why couldn't our kids' careers be much more self-actualizing and fulfilling or contribute far more to society with a little vision and financial help from us?

Take the time to notice what your kids really excel at. What they really enjoy. Be open to new ideas for careers and lifestyles, as they are a new generation with new visions and talents. They typically understand the new technologies and the network world much better than we do. Challenge them to take on responsibilities and don't plan or do everything for them. If you make life too easy for them, they will not develop self-esteem from their own accomplishments and decisions to move into their highest life goals. Let them make their own mistakes within parameters. Don't chastise them, but support them when they make such mistakes and help them to learn from them and realize mistakes are a natural part of life and creativity. Give them more freedom and support if they show they can take on more responsibility. Withdraw that support temporarily if they don't show signs of responsibility and want to retreat into their failures instead of learning from them and moving on. But also be a mentor and contribute your life experience and lessons to help them on their journey without requiring that they do things exactly the way you did.

An Ethic of Contribution

The real flowering of the self-actualization stage comes from using your talents to contribute the most to others and society, including your own family. That is truly a higher goal and source of fulfillment than merely enjoying and showing off your own success in the self-esteem stage. It's not that we don't deserve the latter up to a point, but how fulfilling is it really? Remember the line in *The Scrooge* when the ghost of the future proclaimed to Ebenezer, "You could be the richest man in the graveyard"! Or as I once heard someone put it, "What's the point of being rich if you can't be an asshole?" It's when you suspect you are being an asshole and that merely accumulating wealth and a comfortable environment isn't enough in life that you are approaching the self-actualization stage. What do you think the happiness rating would be on those super-frugal "millionaires next door"?

A friend and fellow speaker and researcher, Layne Longfellow, was the first I heard to call for "an ethic of contribution." Why should people accumulate wealth and power merely to exploit other people? Why should we build and run huge corporations just for the goal of creating the most profits? It's not that corporations don't need profits to sustain themselves, reward their shareholders, and make investments for the future. But is profits really a satisfying and meaningful rallying cause for your employees or customers? . . . "Oh, I'm working for this corporation because our goal is to make $X million by the year 2000." People get the greatest satisfaction from helping other people and making a real difference. You will find a much higher happiness and fulfillment quotient in these people than in the Ebenezer Scrooges of the world.

In this new era of prosperity, as more of us achieve the financial resources to provide for our own needs, we are going to have greater freedom to focus on the human activities that really count and create a higher level of satisfaction, especially as computers take over more and more of the bureaucratic and technical tasks. I see the ethic of contribution growing in a significant percentage of the most successful entrepreneurs and aging baby boomers and across all segments of our society. This urge is most likely to show itself more fully in the midlife crisis that sets in shortly after the kids leave the nest or you achieve the pinnacle of success in your career or get that perfect house and realize that it isn't enough. This principle of self-actualization was perhaps characterized best by John F. Kennedy in his famous quote: "Ask not what your country can do for you. Ask what you can do for your coun-

try." Change country to world or community, and you have a real vision
of how to shape your future.

A Great Era of Philanthropy Ahead

Baby boomers are going to be moving at the highest growth rates
into their late forties and fifties in the coming decade. They are going
to be entering the midlife crisis en masse. Combine this with the fact
that there are more millionaires and multimillionaires being created at
a relative level by this incredible boom than at any time in history. I
can come to only one conclusion. We are going to see the urge for self-
actualization and the ethic of contribution combine to create the
greatest era of philanthropy in history. So don't feel that you are weird
if you are starting to get this urge.

The number of households with a net worth of $5 million or
more was 500,000 in 1995, with an average net worth in that category
of $11.3 million. The number of these households roughly quadru-
pled from 1992 to 1996. That is enough wealth to live off and make
some healthy contributions financially and personally to some serious
causes. According to the same Federal Reserve statistics, the number
of households that had a net worth of $2.5 million to $5 million in
1995 was also 500,000. And the number of households over $1 million
in total was 3.5 million. I would estimate that, as of 1999, that number
has already grown to something like 6 million. That is a combined net
worth as of 1995 of over $10 trillion. And it will probably move closer
to $20 trillion by 2000! Can we change the world with that type of pri-
vate wealth?

And what about the incredibly concentrated wealth that has been
amassed by the entrepreneurs who have created this information revolution and a new economy of products and services? We've almost certainly created more billionaires, adjusted for population and inflation,
than at any time in history. What happens when Bill Gates and
Michael Dell hit their midlife crises and realize there may be an even
greater purpose to life and have possibly hundreds of billions of dollars
that they couldn't spend on themselves, even if they tried? Many people are asking why they haven't already contributed much more. The
reason is they have yet to build their companies to have the greatest

impact on our society—an all-consuming task that we should hope they continue to focus on until they reach their peak contribution. That is more the self-esteem stage. It is when they have maximized those efforts and truly have the time, resources, and freedom to focus on their higher goals and those of society that many of these great entrepreneurs will have their greatest impact on society—in their self-actualization stage.

This is precisely what occurred in the later stages of the last economic revolution. The Rockefellers, Carnegies, Mellons, and many of the new super-rich dedicated the last part of their lives to giving their unprecedented wealth back to society, creating public and private foundations that have survived to present times. This would not have been the expectation when these business titans were absorbed ruthlessly in building the strongest monopolies possible, even blowing up the competition in Rockfeller's case. Who would have thought that these apparent Scrooges would ever become the greatest philanthropists in history?

Most charities I have seen need organizational, professional, and entrepreneurial skills far more than they need money. They have great ideals, but they often don't have the ability to create results as many business people do. Layne Longfellow always questioned why the people with the greatest sense of "cause" couldn't hook up with people who had the greatest capacity for "effect" or why most had to fall into one or the other of these camps. Is it impossible for these two personality traits to appear in the same person? Or, at least, can't these two types realize that they need each other and that the world needs them to work together, not apart? It is my experience that cause and effect do tend to merge in the self-actualization stage. That is the very essence of this stage of human development. You achieve higher levels of personal satisfaction by expanding your horizon beyond your needs for family and personal achievement into an identification with the broader needs of society. You expand your awareness to that greater need and level of existence. You become that and thereby become greater. We are already seeing people like Ted Turner call for the wealthy in the world to contribute more to the greater good.

I think our nonprofit sectors are going to be the greatest growth sector of our economy in the coming decades, especially after the boom ends around 2009. And I think these institutions are going to get both cause and effect when many of our best entrepreneurs and professionals get the urge for an ethic of contribution. The greatest reason this is destined to occur is because so many people in this massive generation will have fulfilled the self-esteem stage due to the incredible advances in prosperity in this boom. Billionaires and multimillionaires aren't the only ones who can create effective charitable causes. Such causes have always been most sustained by the donations and volunteer time of many people. And some of us are going to dedicate our full-time efforts to charity once we graduate from the career and family stage of life.

So don't limit your aspirations only to starting your own business or living in your own paradise. Consider how you can use your highest visions, skills, and resources to make a real difference in this world. This new age of philanthropy is likely to be characterized by many small, focused nonprofit causes that emerge from the visions of individuals and small groups, most often in local areas of influence that will ultimately network and unite in many complex ways. That is the essence of networks. And we will see more businesses realize that it is in their best interests not just to advance the wealth of their shareholders but to create a real contribution to consumers and society that will, in turn, reward their shareholders with customer loyalty and profits.

Great Causes and New Businesses Arise from Individual Experiences

We have all had intense experiences in our lifetimes when a helping hand from someone at the right time made a major difference for us or for others or when a major injustice greatly disrupted our lives or those of others. This can be the origin of philanthropic causes, large and small. What experiences have impacted you or people close to you the most in your lifetime? Did someone you know get injured or die because of a drunk driver? Is there a loophole in the legal system that caused you or your family or your business a great injustice? Did someone you love die from a health problem that could have been prevented? Did the lack of a small amount of funding set back your successful business innovation many years that were unnecessary? Are there products or services that you need that no one is providing?

Did a person or organization give you information, advice, or a challenge at a critical time in your life that caused you to make a major life change for the better? Were you poor but found a way to succeed despite the odds, an insight you could bring to others? Did you find something inspiring that helped you greatly increase the quality of your life or the lives of people close to you? Do you have talents in business that could greatly increase the effectiveness of causes you admire? Or what new causes have you seen that are actually working but critically need funding or skills to expand? Would your talents help launch a new product or service that you and people like you see is needed?

The list of unique experiences, of course, is unlimited. The real question is what has your unique experience taught you that works in life or doesn't work? You can create a business or a nonprofit cause, or you can work for or contribute to a business or nonprofit cause that magnifies your own experience of what could change in this endlessly imperfect world. Don't wait to do this any longer than your practical circumstances require. If you have achieved the capacity for self-esteem and effectiveness, then move on and contribute to greater causes than your own needs, now that you have fulfilled those and are in a position to truly contribute more broadly. You will likely feel much better if you do.

I am not a conservative or a liberal on social issues. Liberals tend to think that you can throw large amounts of money from centralized government programs that often have little effect or accountability for real results. Conservatives tend to want to retreat to the programs and morals of the good old days or to simply rely on the primitive law of "the survival of the fittest." If people can't cut it, let them starve and get them out of the way. I think that as human evolution evolves, we can create new morals and new laws, higher than in the natural world of animals and plants. I think that, much as parents support kids as they develop from lower skills and capacities to higher, the wealthy and more skilled in our society can help to bring up the skills and standard of living of the less skilled—without merely exploiting them. Do we look to exploit our kids just because we have more skills and power than they? Or do we look to help them surpass our skills and quality of life?

In a great example of very practical philanthropy I read about, a successful corporate executive retired by forming a nonprofit organization that simply lent small amounts of money to people in less-developed countries for things like buying a cooler to increase their street sales of drinks. These individuals were required to pay back the small loan out of their proceeds (if at all possible), and that money was then lent to other needy individuals. This cause was obviously based on the wisdom "Don't give people a fish but instead teach them how to fish." This very successful and growing foundation gave people help when needed but also taught them how to expand their business and develop credit in simple ways that they could understand and accomplish.

Obviously, anyone who paid back a loan and had a new plan for expanding his or her business was given another one. Eventually, such a person might build a small business that could even be financed by a small bank and perhaps employ other people or family members. This cause had great effect and used its resources very efficiently, hence magnifying its effects. The payback rate on those loans (which commercial banks wouldn't even touch) was over 95%!

This nonprofit organization could have been set up as a business and been profitable. There are many businesses that need to be created, beyond the scope of large corporations, that could thrive on your personal vision and skills and contribute new products and services that simply don't exist. It is becoming harder and harder in the new economy to distinguish between businesses that thrive on personal vision and cause and nonprofit organizations. This is because the new ethic of self-actualization increasingly blends the two motives, cause and effect, meaning and profits.

The new generations, from the baby boom to generation X to the new millennial generation (often called generation Y or the echo baby boom), have the potential to cause the greatest shift in human evolution in history. Throughout history—and I invite you to study it carefully if you have the time—people with power and resources have tended to exploit those with less power and resources, including animals. Such ruthless techniques of building power have ultimately, over decades to follow, advanced technology and skill access and the standard of living for all over time. But such an approach represents a survival urge at worst and a vulgar approach to building self-esteem at best.

The most successful and capable in this incredible era of prosperity should lead in the creation of this new ethic of contribution and self-actualization. And it can occur only as the new generations move into their "power years" of affluence and influence. For the first time, such a movement to raise all boats in society will not have to come almost entirely from a large, bureaucratic, and parental government. The rise of unions and the New Deal in the 1930s with the goal to redistribute income and create a safety net for the disadvantaged in our society occurred out of the reactions of the average worker and voter to the excesses of the wealthy in the Roaring '20s.

This time it should first come from the vision and good intentions of many resourceful individuals who prospered in this era. And then government, in a more decentralized, network approach, can follow and help set standards and give support, incentives, and public education to support these private efforts. We don't have to go down in history as the next affluent society to exploit its workers and other, less-developed nations. Is that what you would want to look back on from your deathbed? To be Scrooge or not to be Scrooge . . . that is the question. Think about it.

Obsolete at 40?

There is another trend that should force us all to reconsider our life strategies for work and contribution before or just as our kids leave the nest. Thanks to the rapid advances in technologies, skills, and business models, we have a unique development. Younger people increasingly have the advantage in the workplace. They have always been more innovative, but the fact that we gain experience as we age has made workers in their forties and fifties the most productive and highest paid in the past. And in more ancient cultures the elders had extraordinary power and respect due to their great experience and wisdom.

But that is less and less the case. Things are changing so fast that the innovation factor counts far more and our past experience often starts working against us in the workplace as we age. That means younger workers are often promoted faster and are preferred even in key positions. Why not let them do the "heavy work of production and technological innovation" and let aging workers focus more on the functions that require more vision for changing society in more meaningful and human ways? That will be the new definition of wisdom: the ethic of contribution that comes with experience and growth into the higher self-actualization stage of life, not merely the technical and professional skills and self-esteem in the career-building cycle.

The cover article for the February 1, 1999, issue of *Fortune* was entitled, "Finished at 40"! Many highly educated professional workers are being seen as obsolete and are having a hard time finding new jobs in corporations. Again, instead of seeing this as a threat or a bad sign, see it as a clear signal to redesign your life and career earlier than our parents did. This is a great time to start your own business or a nonprofit cause, to consult on a part-time basis to your corporation, or to become an experienced mentor for a younger, more innovative replacement in your arena. Or to move into a more visionary long-term role in your company and let the young Turks take on the administration and implementation tasks. This frees you up to move into the self-actualization stage of life even earlier. Shouldn't that be considered a luxury, not a disadvantage?

Life and work are changing and advancing at the greatest pace in history. To resist these changes is only going to create greater pain and difficulty. Take a pro-active stance instead. Decide today how you are going to create the lifestyle you've always wanted but didn't think was possible. Add color to your life; don't try to stay in black-and-white just because it's familiar, like the 1950s town in the movie *Pleasantville*. This doesn't mean making irresponsible decisions or throwing your life to the wind. It simply means allowing personal vision to drive your life, being open to change, taking calculated risks, and tolerating the inevitable mistakes that come with "going with the flow" and learning from them. That is how we grow and evolve and how our quality of life has improved over time.

Taking calculated risks within a clear but open vision rather than planning everything to the infinite detail is the secret to success among the best entrepreneurs and leaders I have observed. There are many predictable trends to help us create our visions and navigate better, as I covered in previous chapters. But there are also many unexpected challenges that will naturally come in a time of accelerating change. That is why we must be more visionary and open than in the past.

There is another critical trend that we can see coming that not only will affect our businesses and nonprofit causes but will change our cost and quality of living in the future. Inflation rates are going to be very low and relatively flat for the next decade. Then the cost of living and doing business will fall substantially for the first time since the 1930s on the 80-year or two-generation cycle I covered in Chapter 1. We have been told all our lives to protect ourselves against inflation. Now we have to adapt to a new era of deflation after 2009. Shouldn't lower costs of living be better? I will discuss how to leverage that trend despite a declining overall economy in the next chapter.

CHAPTER 6
Deflating the Inflation Myth

WE SURVIVED the greatest inflationary era in history from the late 1960s into 1980. It resulted from the greatest worldwide population advance in history, especially since World War II. Inflation has always followed strong surges in births and population growth because young people have to be supported at great expense as they grow and learn, not only by their parents but also by their communities and government for education. As they finally enter the workforce, they become productive and contribute to society as workers and consumers, bringing inflation rates back down. Even as they enter the workforce, businesses initially have to make huge investments in office or industrial workspaces and training and equipment for them. And such young innovators bring many new technologies, products that society and businesses have to invest in long before they become productive. I discussed this concept briefly in Chapter 1.

But since 1980, when inflation peaked at the highest rates in history as the peak of the baby boom generation entered the workforce, we have seen declining inflation rates, despite outmoded economic theories that say that a growing economy creates inflationary pressures. Economists also say that growing government deficits cause inflation, but we have seen lower inflation since 1980 despite the highest government deficits in our history into 1992. Obviously, economic theories about inflation are not accurate. In fact, they are nowhere close to reality.

I have tried to make economics and investing very simple up to this point. And now I am going to ask you to endure an equally simple and brief look at thousands of years of history. Why? To gain an even greater understanding of why we are in the greatest boom in history, why we had such high rates of inflation in the 1970s, why inflation is so low today, and why we will begin to see falling prices, or deflation, about a decade from now. Simply think of this as the easiest history lesson you've ever received, one that could allow you to have a much better perspective on how we create wealth and increase our standard of living over time.

My extensive studies of history have helped me develop some very simple theories for understanding economics from a new perspective. The first major insight I had from studying thousands of years in great detail was that great inflationary periods almost always seem to coincide with the emergence of powerful new technologies—from the stirrup, horseshoes, and saddle in the late 900s, to the printing press, long-range sailing ships, and gunpowder in the late 1400s, to the steam engine in the late 1700s and the information revolution of recent times. I showed in *The Roaring 2000s* how such major innovations tend to occur to the greatest degrees on approximate 500-year cycles and to lesser degrees on 80-year cycles.

In more recent times, there was a great surge in inflation around the emergence of the steam engine and the Industrial Revolution in its earliest stages in Great Britain in the late 1700s. There was another inflationary period from the very late 1800s into the early 1900s with the emergence of electricity, the phone, and the automobile. And again inflation roared to extremes in the late 1960s and 1970s with the early emergence of personal computers and the present information revolution.

When population surges, it is inevitable in the early stages that the increase in rebellious and innovative new young people will cause both rising expenses and increasing social and technological innovations. These new innovations are also expensive and require massive new investments in infrastructures at first. Therefore, you would expect inflation to follow population increases at a time when such young people and their innovations enter the workforce, then for the economy to boom as they age into inevitable worker productivity and as consumer spending cycles stimulate growth and expansion. Those very productivity advances would then cause the rate of inflation to fall, even as demand and growth surge. That is why great boom periods throughout history have not been inflationary as a general rule.

The early 1800s, following the Industrial Revolution, saw high growth rates with falling inflation rates followed by low inflation rates. The boom period from the mid-1860s into the early 1880s, following the inflationary period into the Civil War, saw similar trends in inflation: first falling, then stable. The Roaring '20s, following the inflation period into World War I, was accompanied by falling inflation rates into 1922, then roughly zero inflation rates into 1929, despite incredible growth in the economy. The booming '50s and '60s saw inflation rates of 0% to 2% after the brief inflationary period into and just after World War II. Now we have seen dramatically declining inflation rates from 1980 into 1998, despite a very booming economy indeed. I am projecting that we will see low, relatively flat rates of inflation over the coming decade.

In *The Great Wave* (Oxford, 1996), David Hackett Fischer shows with the best academic research available how inflation has followed population trends by a slight lag over history. He cites numerous periods of population growth in different areas of the world and shows how inflation followed or accompanied such eras. But he didn't really put the big picture fully in perspective, as the next chart does.

Chart 6-1, compiled by Edwin S. Rubenstein at the Hudson Institute, shows the best estimates of long-term trends in population growth on a logarithmic or ratio growth basis, as I used for my Dow channel in Chapter 1 (Chart 1-2, page 27). This puts longer-term trends in better perspective. This chart also shows the normal numerical population trends that have been exponential or straight up since the mid-1700s. The purpose of ratio graphs is to turn exponential long-term growth paths into linear trends that we can better understand. Therefore, I would advise focusing on the more stable logarithmic or ratio line in the chart.

What we see is that the population growth in the world first started accelerating from the farming revolution back many thousands of years ago to the incredible prosperity of the Greek and Roman times from about 600 B.C. into around A.D. 400. Then population growth

6-1. The History of World Population Growth

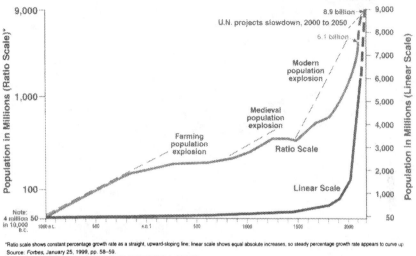

*Ratio scale shows constant percentage growth rate as a straight, upward-sloping line; linear scale shows equal absolute increases, so steady percentage growth rate appears to curve up.
Source: *Forbes*, January 25, 1999, pp. 58–59.
Research: Edwin S. Rubenstein, research director, Hudson Institute, Indianapolis.
Data: Colin McEvedy and Richard Jones, *Atlas of World Population History*; U.N. Secretariat, *World Population Prospects: The 1998 Revision*; Census Bureau.

slowed into the Dark Ages, or from the 500s into the 900s. Population growth surged again from around 1000 into around 1300 and then slowed for more than a century into the mid-1400s. Population growth surged again from the late 1400s into the early 1600s and then slowed again temporarily. It began to accelerate at an even greater level from the mid-1700s into the present incredible modern era of growth. Population growth has accelerated at the greatest rates in history since just before and after World War II—the massive baby boom generation around the world.

> The insight here is simple and unequivocal. When population grows, technological innovation and economic advances follow. The greatest economic and cultural eras of advancing civilization have occurred in periods of rising population growth. When population growth rates slow, economic and technological growth rates decline, as does our standard of living. Most of our dark or disastrous eras have occurred in periods of slow or declining population growth.

If inflation follows periods of population growth and hence is a leading indicator of the growth of our economy, there should be a correlation between rising inflation rates over time and our standard of living. Chart 6-2 demonstrates that relationship with very rough measurements of inflation that I made painstakingly by studying thousands of pages of history and documenting rough increases in inflation rates over 3,000 years, since the early stages of the emergence of Greece and Western civilization.

Economic growth rose into the late 400s (the collapse of the Roman empire). Then both growth and inflation declined into the Dark Ages, until around A.D. 1000. Note that this is not intended to be a concise estimate of inflation in these very hard to estimate past eras. It is simply the best estimate that I could make from compiling the increases in general prices that historians noted over time. When I first compiled these data in the mid-1980s, I had no preconception of what the data would say or how the trends would turn out. But the resulting graph painted a picture of the same four-stage economic life cycle that my previous research had already uncovered for

6-2. Estimated Price History Since Greek Times

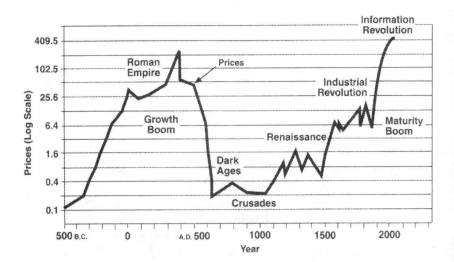

products, technologies, and the 80-year economic cycle documented in Chapter 1.

There was an innovation period from early Greek times, around the 1000s B.C. into the late 300s B.C., followed by a growth boom from around the early 200s B.C. into the A.D. 400s. Then there was a mid-stage shakeout, or deflationary era (the Dark Ages), from the 500s into the 900s. The Crusades around 1000 and then the Renaissance of the 1300s and 1400s ignited the powerful maturity boom of Western civilization, lasting into the present period. Now this approximately 3,000-year civilization cycle is moving toward the East, first to Japan and now to Southeast Asia.

In *The Roaring 2000s*, I pointed out that the peak of civilization has moved over history from East to West. From the great Middle Eastern civilizations and Persian empires to Greek civilization to the Roman empire to the rise of western Europe to eastern North America to western North America today, it has taken almost 3,000 years to move through the evolution of Western civilization as the dominant growth factor in history.

Now we are likely moving into a long period of Eastern growth, starting with Southeast Asia and moving toward India and ultimately the Middle East over time. Will it take almost 3,000 years to move back to the Middle East as the dominant area of civilization? That's too far to speculate at this point, but the direction should be clear.

This brings a very radical insight. Population growth and inflation have been leading indicators of growth and prosperity throughout history as far back as I can document it, even roughly. There is a correlation between rising inflation rates over time and greater specialization in skills and division of labor. As we delegate more tasks to new specialists, the costs of products rise, but the value-added from such new services rises even more. We all specialize more and delegate more, raising our standard of living.

Economists have led us to believe that inflation destroys our standard of living and our economy. It is instead simply our economy's means of financing the investment required to advance our standard of living through subsequent rises in productivity. Declines in population growth and deflation have been leading indicators of the worst periods in history, from the Dark Ages in the 400s to 900s in longer-term cycles to the Great Plague in the mid-1300s to the Great Depression in the 1930s in shorter-term cycles in the past century. Should we really be seeing rising inflation and population growth in the world as a threat?

If we look at Chart 6-3, which is an incredible estimate of inflation back 1,000 years in Great Britain, we can see that inflation did rise in general with the great prosperity following the Dark Ages, from around 1000 into the early 1300s. We then saw prices fall somewhat dramatically into the mid- to late 1300s. That was a very bad period, including the Great Plague. But periods of low inflation or mild deflation tend to be the best for stable growth and widespread prosperity, as occurred in the Renaissance period of the late 1300s and 1400s.

Then we saw inflation and prosperity pick up from the late 1400s into the early 1600s. This was a time when we saw the discovery of America and the rest of the world, the explosion of the scientific revolution, and an expansion from the Mediterranean world to world markets. This is the most similar period to the information revolution and world expansion we are witnessing today. But the period that followed

6-3. Inflation in Great Britain over 1,000 Years

Source: E. H. Phelps Brown and Sheila V. Hopkins.

into the mid-1700s was a more difficult era of slow growth as population growth and inflation slowed.

We truly entered the modern era in the late 1700s after population growth exploded to the greatest degree in measured history. It should be no surprise that economic and technological progress has accelerated ever since. It began with the printing press and then the Industrial Revolution. It grew with railroads and telegraphs, then began to accelerate with telephones, electricity, and automobiles, and now has exploded with computers and the second information revolution, which is just moving mainstream from the late 1990s into the Roaring 2000s.

However, it is also clearly true that rapid population growth and economic advances can ultimately lead to environmental disasters, such as the Great Plague in the mid-1300s, which followed the population surge from the 1000s through the 1200s shown in Chart 6-1 (page 159). In that era there was a massive movement of people into towns and cities from rural areas. The lack of planning for handling sewage and waste products eventually laid the foundation for the rapid spread of the Great Plague. That caused the population to contract into the late 1300s, with dismal economic times and deflation as a result. The lesson here is equally clear.

> If we don't make the investments to deal with pollution and environmental degradation in an era of rapid population and economic growth, we will pay the price into the late stages of the boom and after. In fact, such environmental disasters contribute to the peaking of population and economic growth.

I am not a liberal or a conservative when it comes to these issues. Liberals tend to think that the only solution to the environmental issues of this era is to retreat to the past of living more simply and making clear attempts to slow population growth. The conservatives tend to promote expanding growth and technological progress without attention to environmental issues. The truth is that new technologies and approaches to living hold the secret to solving environmental problems.

New technologies can greatly reduce the environmental impact of past technologies. Most people don't realize that the greatest sources of pollution in the early 1900s, before the car revolution, were horse manure and the smoke from wood and coal burning. Cars were seen as very-low-polluting transportation devices compared to the horse and buggy. Oil was cleaner-burning than coal. It was the saturation of cars, modern machinery, and appliances of the last era that finally made them the new polluters.

Now information technologies can allow us to expand our standard of living again with lower energy and pollution rates in comparison with GDP or economic growth. We can drive many more miles on the same gallon of gas. And hydrogen fuel cells may make cars almost nonpolluting in the future. New business methods will allow us to have a few UPS and Federal Express trucks deliver most of our basic goods to our doors instead of us driving many more miles individually to shop and pick them up. Businesses are operating far more efficiently with lower inventories and energy costs. Waste and unnecessary human bureaucracy are being eliminated at increasing speeds. Recycling is becoming more attractive and is being mandated by government programs. For the first time in decades, air quality is improving in the worst urban areas, like Los Angeles.

The movement to exurban and resort areas allowed by the expansion of information and communication technologies will spread our population over greater areas, as the movement to the suburbs did from the Roaring '20s on. This will allow many of us to experience less congestion, lower exposure to pollution, and greater intimacy in living. No one would have thought that possible in the high-inflation, high-pollution scare of the late 1970s. The truth already is that new technologies and an increasing sensitivity to the environmental excesses of the past industrial age are improving the environmental quality of life as well as the overall standard of living in very developed countries like the United States.

But economic growth will cause even these less-polluting technologies and business methods to cause greater overall pollution if we don't invest sufficiently to offset their effects. That is not as likely as most people think to become a major problem in North America, Europe, Japan, Australia, and New Zealand in the coming decade. The biggest threat from pollution is already exploding in emerging third world countries, which are expanding into industrialization at faster rates with larger populations than we did in the last century. That is where we should be the most concerned.

These countries care much more about their economic progress than about the environmental impact of such growth, just as we did at the same stage of our development in the last century. I think that one of the greatest global political issues in the coming decade will be that the more-developed countries start demanding that emerging third world countries meet increasing pollution standards as a requirement for expanding trade with us. That will be a positive development from my point of view. But it will be important that we make investments from our growing national and worldwide GDP to deal with the impact of waste products and business process design if we are to continue to make economic progress without reducing the quality of our standard of living. This will also entail better zoning and design codes for residential and commercial development to increase aesthetics as well as reduce pollution impact. As population density increases, our own personal, commercial, and governmental expansion impacts us all in more ways. We must plan for this at all levels. In an increasingly decentralized world of decision making and free-market economies, the role of local, national, and global government agencies will have to increase in this arena. Setting standards is the most appropriate role of central governments in a network age of decentralization.

Now, what is the point of taking you through all of this history that you thought didn't have that much relevance to our current era and your life or business? Population growth and inflation have accelerated to the greatest extremes in history since World War II. That means there will be growing prosperity and economic growth for many decades to come, as population is expected to continue to increase dramatically well into the twenty-first century, but this growth is likely to be at a decelerating rate as third world countries industrialize and experience lower birth rates per capita, as we have. And the more-developed countries, led by Europe and now North America, will continue to experience lower birth rates as we prosper and move into the information age.

If we move back from long periods of history to nearer-term trends, we can see that the slowing of birth rates around the world since the peak of the baby boom in the early 1960s in most developed countries (since the early 1970s in many developing countries) has caused inflation rates to fall since the early 1980s. Inflation rates peaked in 1980 in the United States, and as usual, we have seen a very prosperous period of expansion as inflation has slowed.

Despite a continuation of rising inflation over the next century, we are very likely to see a brief deflationary era from around 2009 into the early 2020s on the two-generation or 80-year economic cycle I outlined in Chapter 1, as occurred in the 1930s. That will change everything from investments to cost of living in a very important era of our lives ahead—after the great boom. And yes, there will be another great boom to follow, but it will be centered more in Asia than in North America. And Europe is likely to fall behind more rapidly in that next era.

In Chart 6-4, I am reprinting "The Inflation Indicator" from Chapter 2, page 79, of *The Roaring 2000s* with an update to 1999. I have found that the best correlation with inflation in the current era has been labor force growth on a 2-year lag, as it takes that long for businesses to fully make the investments to expand office space and equipment to accommodate new workers. This indicator, which I first developed in the late 1980s, forecast the decline in inflation since 1980 due to the baby bust generation entering the workforce. It now forecasts that inflation rates will be roughly flat at around 1% to 3% or so into the next decade, as labor force growth is projected to remain slow despite a booming economy. And of course, that means rising wages for workers.

The slow movement of the massive baby boom generation out

6-4. The Inflation Indicator

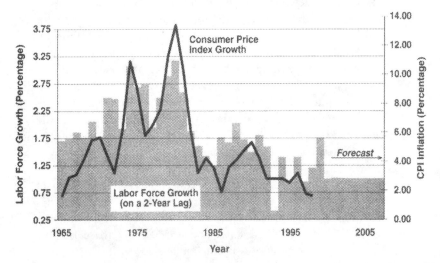

of the workforce, which begins in the late forties, will largely offset the movement of the smaller echo baby boom generation into the workforce from the mid-1990s into around 2009–10. But immigration rates that peaked in 1991 and have been slowing ever since are still a bit of a wild card. If immigration picks up in coming years, as is somewhat likely with our booming economy, inflation rates could rise a bit at times. But such rising rates of immigration would also raise economic growth rates, and that would be positive for the economy overall.

Deflation Is Inevitable after 2009

After this boom ends around late 2008 to mid-2009, deflation in prices is almost certain to ensue for many years to come, likely into the early 2020s. Why? Because economic growth will decline as it did in the 1930s, and there will be a shedding of the excess capacity that came from the great race for leadership in all of the expanding industries into 2009, 80 years after it occurred in 1929. Productivity from the new technologies will still be advancing, unlike in the 1970s, when the last economic revolution was waning. But demand will be falling. This will create deflation in prices. I already discussed how to shift your investments from equities to long-term, high-quality bonds and successively into selective Asian and other international equities that will continue to have strong demographic spending waves. And after we see a major stock crash in the United States, around 2014 to 2016, small company stocks here will be a great investment.

But the biggest trend should be obvious. The cost of living, interest rates, and the price of real estate should drop substantially, as they did in the Great Depression, but not likely to the same extremes. We won't see as dramatic a decline in our economy because the demographic decline is not forecast to be as steep as in the early 1930s. And the slow, continued expansion of parts of Europe, Australia, and New Zealand and the stronger growth in areas of Asia like Japan, China, South Korea, and Thailand and in many parts of Latin America will offset our domestic decline to some degree through export opportunities. I am expecting unemployment rates at the worst to be more like 15% or a little higher, not the 25% we saw at the depths of the Great Depression. But that would still be worse than the 10% unemployment rates we saw at the end of the last inflationary downturn cycle, which bottomed in late 1982 to early 1983.

What Will Your Life Look Like in the Next Depression?

The economy will be bad. Jobs will be harder to find. Many of the most successful businesses in the Roaring 2000s boom will be faltering. The businesses that dominated their markets by the top of the boom will survive the best after drastic restructuring. They will gain market share, as General Motors did in the 1930s when many competitors folded. If you are in a strong employment position with such a company, you will likely do well. Remember that even if there is a 15% unemployment rate, 85% of us will still be employed. And companies don't tend to cut the salaries of the best employees they retain. They cut costs by eliminating unnecessary employees. But salary raises are likely to be a bit harder to come by.

New workforce entrants, the late edge and declining tide of the echo baby boom generation, will have a very tough time getting a job unless they have strong skills. Better to advise your kids to enter the workforce before the boom ends in 2008–9 to gain experience and secure a job and perhaps defer higher education until the bust period, when opportunities will be less forthcoming and the costs of education lower.

The Upside to the Bust

But there are real opportunities in the next deflationary period. A new generation, the one already changing youth trends in fashion, threatening baby boom brands like Levi's and Nike, will make changes and create new brands in other industries as they age. Many new business opportunities will emerge, increasingly favoring smaller companies and entrepreneurs that can identify the new niche markets and respond faster than larger companies. You could be one of those entrepreneurs, whether young and innovative or older with more resources and experience.

Having financial wealth and an open eye for changes in your industry will be invaluable. Look at the new needs of the massive midlife to retiring baby boom generation and the new young echo baby boom generation. Look to new advances in technology, which surge in down economies like the 1930s and 1970s, to spot new opportunities. Be ready to shift your career and lifestyle strategies radically if necessary. Plan for this inevitable transition in our economy in advance and you will prosper, perhaps even more than in the great boom. I once read that more millionaires per capita were created in the Great Depression than at any other time in history.

If you are in the real estate industry and the overall housing market is declining, why not focus on the rising demand for exurban real estate in resort areas and for retirement housing for the baby boomers? Or you could buy distressed residential real estate in the crash, fix it up, reposition it, and resell it in the recovery. In every industry and profession there will be new opportunities as the older sectors decline, just as occurred in the entrepreneurial revolutions in the 1970s and 1930s.

The cost of living will actually decline for the first time since the 1930s. That means that the living costs just before and into retirement for many baby boomers will be much lower than has been projected by many economists and financial advisors. The costs of college for your kids in this era will be falling, not rising. The costs of health care will be falling, and many new innovations for extending our life expectancy and quality of life will just be emerging. Some of those costs may not be falling because of baby boomer demand as they age and need high-impact health services for cancer and heart disease, but they won't be rising as they are today.

Housing prices will drop dramatically, and you will be able to buy almost everything at a lower price if you have money to spend or good credit. And those of us who have built our financial resources in the great boom and those who are still employed will have the money. You will be able to refinance your mortgage at a substantially lower rate, perhaps as low as 3% to 4% for 30-year rates. That could lower your mortgage payments by 30% to 40%. Even if you decide to keep your house and not sell by 2008, your payments will drop dramatically. If you do sell your house before this boom peaks, you can buy a new one at a much lower cost and finance it at much lower interest rates. So you can see why it's important to build your financial assets in this great boom, to switch your investment strategies ahead of the bust, and to secure your career position or start your own business or nonprofit foundation ahead of time.

We have been told for years that health care costs are going to escalate into our retirement, as health care has been one of the highest inflationary factors in our economy. But since the early 1990s the inflation in health care costs has been dropping dramatically back toward the overall inflation rates in our economy, as we can see in Chart 6-5. HMOs started the trend down, often at the expense of our choice. But the next stage of the network revolution will increase the service we get and decrease costs further by radically reducing unnecessary bureaucracy and layers of distribution. A new bottoms-up browser/server model of health care, in which more specialized doctors (browsers) represent unique segments of patients and coordinate insurance and transfer health records to HMOs and specialized health care specialists (servers), will customize our service while reducing costs. Less and less will the government or insurance companies and HMOs dictate our health care choices! We and our doctors will.

6-5. Falling Inflation in Health Care Costs

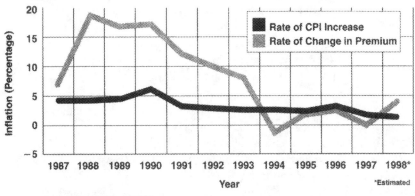

Source: *National Business*, July 1998.
Data: Mercer/Foster Higgins; U.S. Bureau of Labor Statistics.

Health care costs have exhibited higher inflation rates in the past partly because the government is heavily involved and there are so many regulations, rules, and subsidies for the less fortunate that we all have to pay for. All functions that are coordinated by the government tend to be less subject to competition and to be slower to react to the cost-reducing impacts of the powerful information revolution. But there is another reason health care costs have risen faster than the general rate of inflation in the past decades.

This industry has seen massive innovations that have expanded the options we have for improving our health and extending our life span. We should not view this as a burden but as a benefit. It is only natural that, as such quality of life benefits present themselves, we choose to spend a slightly higher percentage of our incomes on such products and services!

Is Inflation Real?

Is inflation really inflation if you adjust for higher quality? Don't our cars have far more options, more comfort, more power, more safety features, and better brakes and stopping distances? Don't we have more choices, from magazines to cable channels to mutual funds to specialty foods and fashion clothing, in this new era? Don't everyday desktop computers have more power than the mainframes of the past? Isn't that worth something? Paul Zane Pilzer, author of *Unlimited Wealth*, makes the point that much of the inflation of the past decades was simply the result of higher expectations by baby boomers and higher quality and choice in products and services. Economists don't measure this accurately, although they make minor efforts to. They measure quantity, not quality, as was consistent with the old standardized economy.

That brings me back to the graph of long-term inflation I presented in Chart 6-3 (page 162). The point was that inflation over time actually represents rising specialization and value-added in the economy and hence greater wealth and a higher standard of living. You can produce and cook your own food, or someone else can specialize and do the job at a higher cost. As everyone specializes more over time through the advance of new technologies and the redesign of work, everyone earns more and can afford to outsource more tasks and enjoy a higher standard of living.

Hence, inflation merely represents a higher level of specialization and a higher standard of living over time. As I pointed out earlier in this chapter, inflation is a leading indicator of progress and standard of living, not a sign of decline and destruction of our economies. It just appears that way in the earliest stages of an economic revolution because we invest more and reap less at first. But we do ultimately benefit, often in direct proportion to the inflation that comes prior to most great boom periods. We could have predicted this great boom without any of the specific indicators in this book, just on the basis of the highest inflation rates in history into 1980!

Education Inflation Rates Will Be the Next to Fall

The one key sector of our economy that is still seeing rising inflation above the norm is education. Government is also involved here, even more strongly than in health care, and that is part of the cause. But we are also seeing constantly rising demand, as we are seeing in health care. Both represent a growing percentage of GDP while many manufactured products and commodities of the past decline in costs. That is natural and desirable. In a rapidly expanding information economy, knowledge and technical skills are in increasing demand. And since it takes longer to educate our young people and the teachers who serve them, you would expect rising costs in education. And then you have to add the increasing demand for adult education as more people have to update skills and switch careers than in the past.

How many families don't value the education of their kids more highly than ever and are willing to spend whatever it costs? And the programs for scholarships from both public and private sources are ever expanding. The percentage of people attending and graduating from high schools, colleges, technical schools, and graduate schools has been increasing constantly over the past century. Isn't this a sign of progress and prosperity? Why do we call it inflation? Why do so many countries, rich and poor, send their best students to our universities?

It is also inevitable that the incredible information revolution will start to rapidly reduce the costs of education in the next decade, just as we have seen in health care in the '90s. The assembly-line revolution of the Roaring '20s rapidly spread from leading-edge manufacturing industries to service industries, including education and government, into the 1930s and 1940s. It made our military supreme in World War II. Mass education exploded from the 1930s into the 1970s. The next stage will bring much more customized and specialized education at all stages of life at much lower costs.

And education will be targeted to our individual needs, delivered much more conveniently over Internet sites where we can access the best experts or teachers through our computers or TVs, just as we can get hundreds of entertainment channels through cable TV or satellite dishes. We will have many more options for accessing live education seminars when we need the direct interaction. The quality of education will go up while the costs go down. But again, our overall expenditures on education and entertainment will rise for the foreseeable future. That is good! That will raise our knowledge as consumers and our skills as workers and entrepreneurs.

Back to the point of planning for our future. Don't believe the estimates of education costs that say that you will have to spend twice as much as today for your kids' college education 10 or 20 years from now. College and private school costs should start to slow in inflation in the next 10 years and then could even decline after 2009—another reason to have your younger kids enter the workforce after high school or college and gain valuable experience and job positioning before going to college or graduate school. The costs and opportunity loss in the job market will be lower after 2009.

The peak in the birth rate of the echo baby boom generation was back in 1990, with a declining birth rate ever since. That means that the peak in demand for college students will be around 2008. After that, there will be declining enrollments and hence greater competition for students and lower costs. That, along with a declining economy, would be the best time to invest in higher education for your kids or for yourself, whatever your age.

Another point I made in *The Roaring 2000s* in Chapter 9 was that kids are taking longer to mature and find their calling in life, as has occurred throughout history as life expectancies and education skills have escalated. More young people are likely to know what they really want to do in life in their late twenties or early thirties. So don't rush them into a career path too early. That doesn't mean they shouldn't work and get practical life experience before that time or that they should stay in school endlessly. It means that they should be allowed to experiment longer and alternate between school and different work experiences until they find their life path.

Advanced schooling amplifies work experience, but real-life work experience also amplifies educational learning and getting a feel for what you are best suited to do in life. It's like buying a shoe without trying it on first to see if it fits. And of course, as we move into multiple career cycles over extended life expectancies and faster learning cycles, we will all have to re-educate ourselves periodically between work cycles. Education and work should become a normal alternating cycle in our lives. Let's start with recognizing this reality for our kids.

This great boom will bring unprecedented opportunities for more people to participate in educational opportunities as well as the equity markets and to leverage their investments in both for the future. You should be targeting today how to build your skills and wealth to a maximum by 2008, before the next great bust. If you systematically build your wealth and knowledge in the next decade, you will have opportunities to adapt to new business, investment, and lifestyle opportunities after 2009. The greatest leverage will actually come in this period if you have the skills, financial freedom, and ability to change your lifestyle and outlook.

In Part 4, I will look at two other critical issues for life and financial planning. In Chapter 7, I will look at how you can find a competent financial advisor who can add far more value than a discount broker in this time of increasingly complex choices and busy lifestyles. Or how to invest optimally if you choose to make your own decisions. You need to get on a systematic plan now to leverage the great boom and to prepare for the great bust. In Chapter 8, I will look at how you can bring tax and estate planning into your wealth-building and life plans. For many, tax efficiency can bring the greatest leverage, and there are many options for deferring or avoiding taxes. Many of them will allow you to contribute back to society in a meaningful way. This may be the new definition of well-being: the ability to have the freedom to contribute your talents and resources to benefit the greater good.

PART 4

Putting Together
Your Financial-Planning
Planning Process

CHAPTER 7

Why You May Need
a Financial Advisor and
How to Find a Great One

IN ALL OF MY BOOKS on investment, I have talked about the importance of having a competent and objective financial advisor. That means someone who represents you, not the investment products. In other words, not a salesperson. That means someone who can integrate your entire financial-planning process, effectively and efficiently, to meet your highest life goals. Before you consider whether you should be investing on your own through a discount broker or using one of many financial advisors, from insurance agents to stockbrokers to financial planners to CPAs to tax attorneys, ask yourself these questions. This may be a bit painful, but it should prove very useful if you will just stick with me for a few pages.

Do you have the discipline, the expertise, and the time to analyze your own financial and life goals and to stick to such a plan? Do you understand insurance and risk management, from home to casualty to auto to disability to life insurance? Do you clearly understand and monitor your fixed annual and monthly expenses, as well as your variable weekly and monthly ones, so that you can reasonably project, manage, and monitor your finances? Including planning for those unexpected contingencies in life, ranging from health crises to auto maintenance to roof repairs?

Do you understand the ever-changing tax laws and how you can best defer taxes or avoid them or plan for them in advance? Do you know what a charitable remainder trust is and how it could give you income for life with tax advantages while benefiting the nonprofit institution you value the most? Would you know how to set up your own charitable foundation that is like an unlimited IRA or 401K plan and draw a salary for life while serving your most cherished causes? Do you know how to roll over your 401K plan when you leave your company and how long you have to do that without losing the tax benefits?

Do you understand how to measure the tax efficiency of a mutual fund or index fund? Do you understand what turnover means and how it affects your taxes from the fund you invest in? Do you know what the current capital gains tax laws are or the advantages of capital gains over ordinary income? Or how long you have to hold an investment to get capital gains advantages? Is it the same for your house as for your stocks? How much can you borrow against your house and still deduct the interest on your tax return? Does this apply to your vacation home? What restrictions are there on that interest deduction if you have a higher income? What is the alternative minimum tax? Are you subject to it even if your income isn't that high?

Do you know what a variable annuity is or what is so variable about it? And how a variable annuity could allow you to never pay taxes on your investment income? Or why it is different from a fixed annuity and what is so fixed about it? What is variable universal life and what does life insurance have to do with deferring taxes or avoiding estate taxes? Do you understand how to evaluate whether a variable annuity has greater advantages over buying stocks or funds and holding them for long-term capital gains? Or how your rate of investment returns in that vehicle, whether higher or lower, affects that decision? Are municipal bonds the best way to avoid taxes just because the interest is tax-exempt? Is that interest tax free for federal taxes or for state and local as well?

Do you understand how to scientifically combine different investments to optimize your returns versus your risks? Do you understand the difference between long-term and short-term bonds or high-yield and low-yield bonds? Are junk bonds as risky as they sound? Are stocks always more risky than bonds? Do you understand the difference between growth and value stocks? Do you know how large a large cap stock is or how small a small cap stock is? Is a mid-cap stock halfway in between? Do you understand when small companies and large companies do better and why? Does the Russell 2000 or the Russell 3000 best measure the performance of small cap stocks? Does the S&P 500 or the Dow best measure the performance of large cap stocks?

Do you know how to evaluate the 9,000-plus mutual funds that are out there? Do you know what a unit investment trust is? Do you understand the specific differences between mutual funds, unit investment trusts, and index funds? We have been told that S&P 500 index funds are beating most mutual fund managers. Has this always been the case? Will it be the case in the future? Everyone wants the highest returns from investing, but do you understand that most of the highest-growth stocks and mutual funds experience the greatest downturns when the market turns sour?

Do you know that many investors who claim they won't sell their stocks or funds in a 10% or 20% correction actually panic and do so? Did you panic between late August and mid-October of 1998 and then miss the incredible rally in stocks that followed? Or did you panic in late 1997 if you held Asian funds? Or in the corrections of 1994 or 1990? Or in the extreme correction of 1987? If you weren't an investor then, imagine that the stock market is down 40% in a matter of weeks and many of the best experts are claiming this is the next 1929 crash. Would you have sold right near the bottom? Or would you have had the courage to buy at that point?

Do you understand how to evaluate the risk or volatility of stocks and mutual funds? Do you know what the Sharpe ratio is and how it measures risk and volatility? Have you ever heard of other risk measures, such as M-squared or beta or standard deviation? How could a deviation be standard? Do high-risk stocks and funds always go down more than the market? Or could they be considered high risk even if they tend to go up more than they go down? Why would you mind if your fund went up most of the time and didn't go down worse than the market when the market did correct? How do you measure that?

When you invest in a large cap value fund or a small cap growth fund, do you understand a concept called style consistency, which measures whether the fund manager is investing in the type of stocks he or she claims to be consistently over time? How do you know what you are investing in when you buy a fund? Would you want to invest in a fund that has a great track record but a new manager? How would

you determine the track record of that new manager or find out if he
or she has a proven track record in past funds? How old is the fund
manager? Are younger managers better than older ones? Are two managers better than one?

Is a five-star fund always the best one to invest in? Should you put
more weight on the 1-year, 3-year, 5-year, or 10-year track record of a
fund? Should you use the ratings of Morningstar, Lipper, or CD
Weisenberger for evaluating mutual funds? Have you ever heard of
CD Weisenberger? Have you measured the fund you are considering
versus other funds in its category for return and risk, or are you just
measuring it versus the S&P 500?

Do you understand the demographic, technology, and political
factors driving most of the booming and busting countries around the
world? Can you even name most of the countries around the world or
their leaders? Is Mark Mobius a movie star who looks like Yul Brynner
or an international fund manager? What is his actual track record, or
do you like him because you've seen him regularly on TV or in magazine ads? Is that a good reason to trust him as an investment manager?
Why are interest rates in Japan so low yet its economy is still slowing?
Could Hong Kong boom even if Japan continues to decline? Will
there be a war between North and South Korea?

What are derivatives? Do you understand how hedge funds often
use leverage and why they got in trouble in late 1998? Did you believe
the news when it said that the failure of such hedge funds could cause
an international crisis in late 1998? If that scared you, did you miss the
incredible rally in stocks that followed such news into early 1999?

Do you understand why stock valuations rise when interest rates
or inflation rates fall? Why does that occur? Aren't stocks just supposed
to measure the future earnings potential of the company? Do you understand the "time value" of money and how future earnings are dis-
counted back to "present value"? Do lower inflation and interest rates
affect large company or small company stocks more? Why would that
make a difference?

Do you understand what the relative strength of a stock or mutual
fund or sector is? Do you understand what accumulation ratings
mean? Who is accumulating and why? Would it matter to you who is
buying a fund or stock, what major funds or institutions, and why is
that important? If large mutual funds are buying a stock, is that a good
sign of momentum or a sign of overvaluation? Do you understand how

liquid a stock is or what "the float" means? It could make a big difference in whether you can easily buy or sell those shares when you need
to! Do you understand what insider trading means and whether it is a
good or bad sign? Do you understand the difference between a market
that is rising with expanding breadth or declining breadth and what
that means?

Do you understand puts and calls or what the put-to-call ratio
means? Is a high put-to-call ratio a good or bad sign for stocks or the
stock market? What are oscillators and what do they mean for signal-
ing when the market may be peaking or bottoming? Is it better to buy a
stock when it is down or when it is soaring? Is value or momentum investing better and in what type of stocks or mutual funds? How do you
measure valuations on stocks? P/E (price to earnings) ratios or price to
sales or price to book value? Are Internet stocks overvalued? Should
valuations today be higher than in the past or is this a sign of the next
great bear market?

What does volume of trading have to do with the prospects for
stocks? Would you rather buy a stock that is breaking above old highs
on lower volume of trading or higher volume of trading? What is high
or low volume in trading, anyway? Is rising volume more important in
downturns or upturns? Is it the volume on the Nasdaq or the New York
Stock Exchange that matters more? What is Elliot wave theory? Is it
more bullish if a stock rises in two waves up or three waves up before
pulling back? What does the Fibonacci ratio say about how far a stock
or stock market index may correct before it advances again? How do
you tell if a stock that is falling is good value for buying or a dog?

**And here's the biggest question if you are making your own in-
vestment decisions. Have you beat the S&P 500 over the past 5
or 10 years?**

Look at your track record in total and objectively. The chances
are very high that you haven't, especially since most professional investment managers have failed to do so. And you are probably investing on a very part-time basis without the leading-edge technologies or
specialization in education and training. If you think you have discount trading costs, think how much lower these high-volume professionals get when they trade.

Do you know the answers to most of these questions? Very likely not! That's why I asked them! The point I am trying to make from extensive experience in the investment industry is simple. Investment and wealth building, although very simple in principle, are almost as complex as health care and medicine. You may be able to understand the simple principles of diet and exercise and become more involved in building your own health. But it takes the expert advice of a doctor and many technicians and experts to back your doctor up. Your doctor is your browser, and all of the experts and medical institutions and suppliers are the servers. Would you want to go to a discount doctor or a discount surgeon if you had a serious heart problem? Would you be likely to know you had a serious heart problem if you didn't go to a specialist?

The financial services industry is a complex, knowledge-intensive industry that has a very high impact on our well-being, almost as much as health care. Therefore, we should take our wealth-building process seriously and not casually assume that we can do it on our own in our spare time—as if many of us have much spare time! If you are investing on your own and making your own decisions, you should first ask yourself if that really makes the most sense. If you are beating the S&P 500 over time *and* you have the competence *and* you enjoy doing this *and* you have the time—then you can follow the principles in this book and proceed ahead. If not, you should consider finding a very good financial advisor, a competent and well-meaning professional.

Note that I am implying that you need one human browser to integrate all of your financial planning needs. If you have many advisors in the different aspects of investing, insurance, taxes, and cash and credit management, then you will not have a coherent and integrated plan. You will instead get many different and conflicting opinions and spend a lot more of your valuable time and money sorting through them.

So that brings up the real question. If you are already working with a financial advisor, does your financial advisor understand all of these issues that I just questioned? The truth is that he or she may not. Are you getting an integrated plan that addresses all of these issues from the different agents you may be working with, from insurance brokers to stockbrokers to tax advisors? Are you getting the education you need to understand the investment process and the service you need when you need it, so you can feel good about it and sleep at night? Are you an important client to your advisor or a not-so-preferred client?

The truth is that the investment profession is like all other professions. There are great advisors, good advisors, not-so-good advisors, and downright scoundrels. There are competent professionals who represent your best interests, and there are salespeople who sell the most products at the highest commissions for them. There are people who specialize and know their clients well, and there are people who try to be everything to everybody. There are people who are motivated only by "knocking off" more clients, "closing them" on a sale, and moving on.

And there are people who act like they are selling you a portfolio for a very low commission or fee and then talk you into a "timing model" to protect you from downturns at an extra 1% to 2% per year. Doesn't that sound like the worst of car dealers, who make you feel like you bought the car near cost and then trick you into a paint protection package for an extra $1,000 that costs them less than $100? Timing models don't work over time. So don't buy them. Or they sell you a variable annuity to reduce your taxes when you are in a low tax bracket or when you have a time horizon for using your funds within five years. These are the scoundrels!

If your advisor or broker doesn't spend sufficient time with you for you to feel good about your investments, if he or she is merely a salesperson, or worse, if he or she sounds like one of the scoundrels, then you should be finding a new advisor. If you don't have an advisor or don't know how to find one, start by asking your friends and business associates about their advisors and why they like or don't like them. The best people to ask are people just like you, people who have similar occupations, income or wealth, goals and lifestyles. Of course, those are the people you are likely already to know. Birds of a feather tend to flock together.

Ask your friends what type of results they have had in investment performance, how competent and objective their advisor is, what type of service they get, how specialized the advisor is, and so on. Does the advisor specialize just in insurance or mutual funds or taxes? Does he or she have a network of other specialists to meet your other needs? How long has the advisor been in business? What is his or her education and experience?

Or look for advisors who educate you first through seminars or newspaper columns or radio/TV shows or educational Web sites. That way you can evaluate their expertise and approach without listening to

a heavy sales pitch. Make them audition or prove themselves before
you have to spend time with them or consider working with them.
Don't respond to invasive cold calls at dinnertime touting extraordinary investment opportunities. Just hang up! The same goes for ads
full of hype and promises for easy returns. Just ignore them! Look for
advisors who have been rated well by objective sources like local news-
papers or national magazines. For example, *Worth* magazine rates the
top financial planners around the country every year.

Ask your CPA or lawyer or tax advisor or perhaps the financial of-
ficer of your company whom they use or would recommend as a financial advisor. Call national or local associations of financial planners
for referrals in your area. Ask for the professional credentials of the advisors they recommend and the length of time they have been in business and for referrals if possible. Visit or call the local office of a
reputable brokerage firm in your area and specifically request a reputable advisor who represents people like you. Make it clear what your
investment resources and goals are and that you don't want their newest,
least-experienced advisor. Demand that you be allowed to interview a
number of advisors, not just the person they want to allocate to you.

Once you finally meet with a potential advisor, here are the questions to ask:

1. **The first key issue: Do you specialize in working with clients
   like me?**
   a. What actual percentage of your clients are people like me?
   b. How does working with people like me allow you to find unique
      and specialized solutions and experts?
   c. Who are the key experts or investment funds and companies you
      work with and how do they meet the needs of people like me?
      How did you select those experts or investment products? How
      long have you worked with them successfully? How well do you
      know these companies and how closely do you work with them?
2. **The second key issue: Do you represent me or the investment
   products you sell?**
   a. Do you sell only your own company's investment products or a
      narrow range of investment products? Why? Is that because you
      have narrowed down the choices to the best for clients like me or
      because you are best rewarded by your company or other vendors?

b. Do you make commissions or loads on the investment products you sell, or do you charge me directly for your services, or both? How much are those commissions or loads if you do charge them? If you do charge commissions or loads, doesn't that give you the incentive to convince me to keep switching investments? Or do you have a clear policy of not doing that unless it is truly in my best interests and you inform me of such commissions and loads in advance? Why wouldn't it be better that you charge me a fee commensurate to your services and not bias you or me toward greater trading and churning?

c. If you don't make commissions or loads, how do you charge for your services? Is it a percentage of my investment assets under management? Or is it an hourly fee, or both?

d. If your fee for management of my investment assets is over 1%, why is it that high? Do you provide extra services, or is my situation complex enough to justify such a fee? Is that competitive with other advisors or firms that provide similar services? Give me clear proof that such is the case.

e. Do you charge lower percentage fees on higher levels of assets? In other words, do I get a discount for being a larger and better client or if I build my account over time? If not, why not? Do you want to risk losing me to another advisor as my account grows?

3. **The third key issue: How long have you been in business?**
   a. What are your educational credentials?
   b. How many clients do you have? What are their average assets under your management?
   c. How much in investment assets would you estimate that you manage in total for all of your clients? How much in assets does your firm have under management?
   d. Can you give me several referrals?

4. **The fourth key issue: How do you market your services?** Through ads, phone marketing, word of mouth, seminars, newspaper columns, radio/TV programs, your Web site, etc.? Let me see examples of your ads, brochures, seminar programs, or other marketing efforts.
   a. What have been your greatest successes with clients like me?
   b. What have been your greatest mistakes, and what did you learn from those failures?

5. The fifth key issue: Will I get the type of service I need from you?
   a. Will I be a priority account for you?
   b. Are you available when I have questions, or who at your office is available for different kinds of questions?
   c. How do you evaluate the investments and tax strategies that are appropriate to my goals and risk tolerance?
   d. How do you update me on market events and changes in your outlook? Through newsletters, phone calls, Web site updates?
   e. How often do we need to meet personally or update over the phone or your Web site?
   f. How often do you issue statements of my account?
   g. Are those statements understandable and make clear my returns and performance versus benchmarks appropriate to my investing style and risk?
   h. How do you plan to rebalance my portfolio as market conditions change or if I am not performing as well as the appropriate benchmarks?
6. The sixth key issue: What is your outlook for the future of investments and why?
   a. What experts do you rely upon to project economic trends, and what credentials and track records do they have? Can you allow me to understand what I am investing in and why?
   b. How do you re-evaluate and change investment strategies as long-term trends are projected to change? How will you position me for this decade, for the next decade, the next down market?
   c. Can you explain to me why and when I am likely to have to make significant changes in my portfolio and tax strategies?
7. The seventh key issue: Can you integrate all of my financial needs into a comprehensive financial plan?
   a. Can you and/or your expert network handle my investment, tax, insurance, cash management, and credit needs (including mortgage, checking, and interest-bearing accounts)?
   b. Can I get all of my financial accounts and reporting on one simple statement?
   c. Is your financial plan presented in a written document?
   d. Is that document long, complex, and hard to interpret—or is it clear, simple, and to the point?
   e. How often do you update my financial plan and under what conditions or key events?

You don't have to ask all of these questions, just the ones most pertinent to your needs and concerns. And don't expect a financial advisor to get a perfect score on this test but to demonstrate from such questions that he or she will represent you and has the competence and specialization to meet your needs. For example, there are still a number of good financial advisors who charge for their services based on the commissions or loads they get from the products they sell. This can result from the relationships they have with the best vendors they have found, or it may be because many of their established clients still prefer that form of compensation. As long as they fully disclose that and pledge to put a long-term approach to investing and your interests first, that can be okay. But you may also ask if they would consider working with you on a fee basis or on a percentage of your assets under management.

Before approaching a financial advisor, be as clear as you can on your own life goals, priorities, and finances. That may mean meeting with a psychologist, mentor, friend, or support group first. It will make the financial advisor's job easier and your desired results clearer. How do you get to where you are going if you don't know where you want to go?

When it comes down to it, you need, at a minimum, a trusted health advisor, a psychologist, and a financial advisor to achieve the lifestyle you want. They should all be specialists or browsers who deal with people like you and can coordinate the expertise of more specialized experts (or servers) when necessary. If they really know their stuff and represent you, then they will be well worth their fees. Remember that history shows that we expand our quality and standard of living by specializing in what we do best and delegating more tasks to specialists who do what they do best.

Doing everything yourself and saving fees is not the road to success or prosperity. This strategy works only when you can more easily do something yourself than someone else can and when the impact is not that great, liking pumping your own gas while you are trapped at the pump anyway. Or having your computer monitor your spending trends and set up your repeat purchases to be delivered directly to your home or office. But there are many areas where we require real human knowledge to sort through the options. I think financial services and investments comprise one of those arenas. And objective surveys of investor performance tend to demonstrate this.

I mentioned the Dalbar study in *The Roaring 2000s*, which showed that the typical investor trading on his or her own greatly underperformed the S&P 500 from 1984 through 1996. But the typical investor using a broker also underperformed nearly as badly. A more recent study from Brad Barber and Terrance Odean from the University of California at Davis showed that the more investors trade, the lower their returns. They analyzed investor returns from 1991 through 1996. They did not find the same underperformance as the Dalbar study, but they did find that for the 20% of investors who traded the most, the return was 11.4%, compared to 17.9% for the S&P 500.

The more convincing data have come from recent studies from Hewitt Associates, a leading 401K plan administrator. Chart 7-1 shows that there was a strong surge in switching from equities into bonds in 401K plans right into the low of the Dow on August 31, 1998. That was a bad decision. And the rapid reversal in the equity markets made it very hard to get back in. Again, although most people answer surveys

7-1. The Hewitt 401K Index

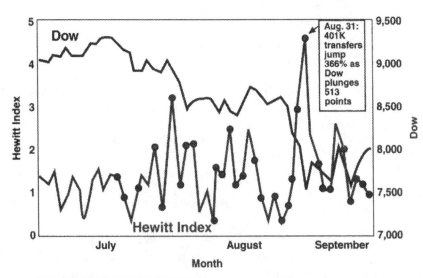

Source: *San Jose Mercury News*, Sept. 20, 1998.
Data: *Hewitt Associates* (www.hewitt.com/401kindex).

claiming that they won't sell in a correction, many of us do when the markets scare us. A 10% correction looks like it will be a 20% correction when it is happening and the bad news is paramount. A 20% correction looks like it could be a 40% correction or perhaps the end of a bull market. All the news worsens as the market is about to bottom, making a reversal back up very hard to detect.

But the most convincing evidence comes from the Brooks Hamilton and Associates analysis of 401K plan activity in 1997. Chart 7-2 measures the average returns of 401K participants in a large plan during 1997, a year in which the S&P 500 advanced 31%. The higher-income participants in the plan did much better than the lowest-income participants! Participants with incomes of $50,000 plus got returns of 26%, 5 percentage points less than the S&P 500, while the lowest-income participants greatly underperformed. People in the $30,000 and lower range made only 6%, 25 percentage points lower!

Why does the more-typical investor so underperform? I would

7-2. 401K Plan Returns by Income Level in 1997

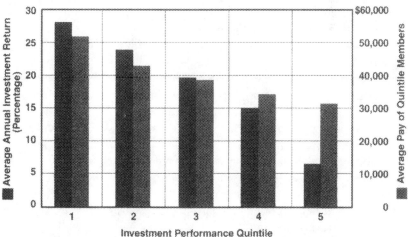

Source: Brooks Hamilton & Associates, Worth, September 1998, p. 118.

give two reasons. Either they trade a lot based on short-term news and trends, or think they have to beat the odds on such low assets to get ahead, as in the "win the lottery" psychology. Or they are scared to death of the markets and perceive equities as too risky and hence choose low-risk bonds and money market accounts. The reality is that the very investors who are told that they are better off trading on their own using discount brokerage accounts or who are encouraged to make their own decisions within their 401K accounts are the ones who most need a systematic plan or a competent advisor. Companies that are trying to avoid the liability of choosing investment plans for their participants by delegating the choices are actually opening themselves to liability suits down the road when their employees aren't prepared for retirement.

What is the solution? We need more advisors who focus on growing the investment assets of the broader population that is investing through pension plans, 401K plans, and individual investment accounts. We need companies to spend more time educating their 401K plan participants on how to invest and even require that they choose a systematic plan that fits their demonstrated risk profile, just as a competent advisor would. How could this happen efficiently? Through educational and easy-to-use Web sites and video/CD-ROM systems that can help employees and less-experienced investors choose a systematic plan. Such a plan does not have to be limited to one or a few mutual fund families or options. It could help select the best funds in the best portfolio strategy for each investor.

Ultimately, I see the emergence, not of online discount trading, but of online advisory services like 1-800-MUTUALS that help everyday investors to evaluate their goals and risk tolerance and to choose a systematic plan that is scientifically determined and rebalanced over time. This will be possible over automated Web sites that allow you to step through a systematic analysis of your needs and risk tolerance, and through videoconferencing with online advisors, which can save costs while still emphasizing a systematic approach and offering human advice when you need it. This is where I see the full-service brokerage firms heading in the next decade. That is what has been proven as the best approach, not only for the wealthy but for the everyday investor who most underperforms in investing. So carefully consider what approach to investing is best for you.

Options for Investing Systematically

Do It Yourself with a Plan and a System

If you think you can time the markets and constantly switch stocks, sectors, and funds, good luck! I just hope you are honest enough with yourself to measure your performance over time and be humbled if you don't turn out to be Warren Buffet. But you may have the discipline to stick to a balanced plan of mutual fund investment over time if you take the initial time to determine your risk tolerance and needs and select good long-term funds for investment. Then you may be fit to use a discount broker and simply buy good funds or index funds in key areas in strong sectors that balance risks, as I outlined in Chapter 2. This would also require that you develop a system of rebalancing periodically or shifting during corrections as well.

Using discount brokers and low-cost index funds can reduce your costs and hence increase your investment returns to a minor degree over time. That can compound and make a difference. But such differences will quickly be erased if you make significant errors, like selling in a correction because you panic or picking a fund that did very well in recent years but then suddenly falters.

If you are a do-it-yourself investor, you are going to see more index funds for investing that focus only on the largest companies in a sector so that you can leverage the continued trend toward larger companies that I documented in Chapters 1 and 2. Then there will be more options for effective investing if you have the discipline and time and if you don't have a complex situation that demands expertise in tax and estate planning and life insurance issues.

Use a Guided Online Service

More discount brokerage firms, as well as traditional full-service firms, will begin to offer Internet sites that have software to guide you through a systematic evaluation of your needs, risk tolerance, and investment objectives. This software will ask you the typical questions that an advisor would, and come up with portfolio recommendations that you can then follow, including highly rated funds in each category in your portfolio to choose from. But it will still be your responsibility to choose your investments and to stick to the plan over time. Like the discount brokerage accounts, such automated plans will not likely be capable of dealing with more complex situations in which tax and estate planning or insurance and risk management are key issues. They will also tend to put you in the same underperforming asset allocation strategies of the past. However, such software systems will get better over time at dealing with such issues to greater degrees. But you may end up being the "guinea pig" until such systems prove capable of dealing with these issues.

The key issue comes down to whether you have the time, discipline, and expertise to make your own decisions. Even if you do have the expertise and discipline, is your time valuable enough to you that you don't want another responsibility or risk to deal with in life? Would it be worth something like 1% of your assets per year to have someone who is a specialist deal with these issues and update your portfolios and planning?

Use a Personal Advisor

A study by Dalbar showed that 89% of people who have more than $100,000 to invest prefer to have a financial advisor. Why? As your financial assets rise, there is more at stake. The costs of making a mistake in investing or overlooking a tax advantage rises. It is also likely that the value of your time is higher and the extra hours per week or month to manage your investments is prohibitive or cuts into the little time you have with your family and hobbies. And the complexity from tax and other risk-management issues rises exponentially with your income and assets. What is 1% of your assets per year when they are growing at 17% or perhaps higher, as I have shown is possible without taking excessive risks in this incredible boom?

You will see a broader array of services in personal advisors. Highly automated plans for people with simple investment objectives and lower assets to invest will become increasingly popular. You will still have a personal advisor who is responsible for rebalancing your account and keeping you informed of key changes when needed. There will be someone you can contact if you have questions, but you won't be able to call every day or you will become unprofitable for the company and show that you can't stick to a systematic plan, even with their help.

New firms like 1-800-MUTUALS are offering managed accounts with a personal advisor for accounts as small as $10,000. They rate and choose the mutual funds in a balanced portfolio and rebalance periodically. They charge 1% of assets under management, which comes to only $100 per year for a $10,000 account. Large brokerage firms are offering more-automated systematic investment plans for smaller investors at lower overall fees, with human advice but less service. The truth is that that is the best approach for smaller accounts that don't have the complexity of tax and other issues. Just put your money in good funds in a balanced portfolio and hold it as long as fundamental trends favor that approach. Trading and worrying about short-term trends only works against most investors.

More and more personal financial advisors will be specializing in the type of clients and the asset ranges that they can best serve. There will be more service and more complexity of options for those who need it and less for those who don't. That is also the way it should be. If you have $50,000 in assets, you are not going to get the same service as someone with $5 million. And you are not likely to need it. If you have very high assets and a very complex tax situation, then you are going to require more interaction with your advisor, and the advisor will have to have more specialized experts to provide services to help meet your needs.

Even more complex accounts will be able to be handled increasingly over Web sites as videoconferencing becomes more commonplace and affordable over the coming three to five years. Your advisor could not only keep you updated on key trends, changes, and opportunities but also pipe in the best experts at his or her firm or throughout the industry to help keep you informed. If the market drops 1,000 points in a week, they will bring in the best economic experts to inform you of why you should be buying, not selling, and where the best opportunities are. They can bring in the best tax experts when the laws have just changed or appear about to change.

The point is simple. You will get the best service and results if you find an advisor and a firm that focuses on clients like you, knows your needs, and meets them effectively in an integrated manner that is cost and time efficient for you. But you have to clearly evaluate your

life priorities and needs first. Then choose an approach to investing
that is consistent and that is based on realistic approaches, not the
hope that you may be the one genius that beats the odds with a novel
approach.

Lifestyle Comes First, Not Money or Costs

The secret to lifestyle is doing what you do best and spending
more time with your family and the hobbies that most reward you. Analyzing the markets and choosing stocks or mutual funds is time-
consuming and takes considerable expertise. If you have the discipline
to choose and stick with a simple plan for investing, then you may be
able to manage this without an advisor. You can follow all the guidelines in this book and other books on financial planning and meet
your goals. For most of us, a competent advisor, online and inexpen-
sive or personal and complex, can make a big difference and save us
much time and agony. Of course, having the right advisor makes all
the difference, both in your investment results and your peace of
mind.

To summarize, I recommend that you take your life planning and
the financial resources necessary to achieve those goals very seriously.
The next decade will allow you to build your wealth and options for
lifestyle more than at any time in history. For the first time in history,
far broader segments of our society have the capacity to participate in
the equity growth of our economy rather than just through wages. We
can choose from many "packaged" investment products—from mutual funds to unit investment trusts to index funds to fixed and variable
annuities—that combine diversification, professional expertise, tax deferral, and lower trading costs. We have pension plans, incentive plans,
401K plans, and all their evolving derivatives, including Roth IRAs.

We need advice from a competent professional to help us sort
through these expanding options, advice that meets our needs at costs
and service levels that are fair and appropriate. We also need to consider the impact of taxes on our wealth accumulation and investment
plans. All of us need to maximize our tax-deductible plan contributions at work or in our businesses. We need to consider tax-deferred
and tax-exempt plans for investing outside those plans. Compounding

investment returns tax free or tax deferred can make a huge difference over time.

There are many conflicting views on taxes that I will help you sort down to the basics that really matter. But the reality is this: Despite a call for simpler tax laws, taxes aren't getting simpler. They are getting more complex as our society gets more complex and income inequality increases during this time of accelerated change. The next chapter isn't about tax evasion. Tax incentives are given to promote the best interests of society. Unintended "loopholes" don't tend to last very long.

You need to look at the full array of options and choose the ones that make the best sense for you and for society. The higher your income, the more options and the more restrictions there are. There are some very interesting options for helping the charitable causes that you favor at a minimum cost to you. That's what I will look at in the final chapter.

CHAPTER 8
The Truth About Taxes

WHY IS TAX PLANNING SO IMPORTANT for more-affluent people? Because they pay most of the taxes! We constantly hear rhetoric about the middle-class tax burden. This simply is not true. The top 1% of income earners, households with incomes above $229,230, paid 32.3% of the federal individual income taxes in 1998. The top 5%, households with income greater than $101,202, paid 50.8%. The greatest federal tax paid by most everyday people is Social Security, but we supposedly get that back with interest when we retire. Although many think that most of us won't get our fair share of Social Security in the future, it is my opinion that most lower-income households will get more than their share and that middle-income households will get most of their share. It will be the affluent, those who paid in the most, who will get rationed out as the system likely converts to paying more by need than by contribution.

Forty-two percent of Americans feel they get their money's worth from federal income taxes, according to a survey from Maritz Marketing Research. I think it is likely that less than 10% of the top 5% who pay the majority of taxes would agree with that statement. Some 56% believe they get their money's worth from state taxes, and 60% feel that way for property taxes. Obviously, the more local the taxes, the more impact and control we feel we have. But the real truth is that taxes fall very disproportionately on the more affluent. They can more easily bear this burden, of course, but it simply doesn't feel good to have 50% or more of your hard-earned income go to taxes, especially when you don't use most of the services, like roads and schools, any more than anyone else and especially when you don't use welfare and social services at all. Most of us who earn more normal levels of income, with tax burdens more like 20% or less, would probably not feel so good about the tax system if we or our kids made $100,000 plus.

So that's the real truth about taxes. We live in a free-market economy that rewards the people who contribute the most, often very disproportionately. And during the early stages of massive changes, this economy is accelerating the income of the rich faster than that of middle- or lower-income households. But we also live in a democratic political system in which everyone gets one vote regardless of income or wealth. And the average voter will choose to place the tax burden on those who can most easily afford it. These two systems, free market and democracy, are typically seen as being similar in nature and structure. They are alike only in that they allow all people to participate. In reality, they operate on opposite principles. One tends to distribute wealth upward, while the other redistributes it downward. The reason they have worked well together throughout history is that they balance each other's effects while encouraging a participatory economy and society.

Many economists and politicians argue that tax policies set by the government can have a huge impact on work ethic and entrepreneurial incentives. That may be true up to a point, but I don't think Bill Gates or Michael Dell was driven or not by the marginal tax rate. However, there is one thing about tax policy that we can document very clearly. Changes in tax rates don't change the level of income collected by the government. That means that higher rates don't decrease motivation to innovate just to avoid higher tax rates. Chart 8-1 (page 198) shows how the taxes taken by the federal government as a percentage of GDP has remained largely constant over the past six decades, despite huge differences in tax policies, from marginal rates of over 70% down to below 40%, and capital gains rates that have varied similarly. The more taxes that are raised, the more they have to be targeted toward the rich, and the more rules and loopholes are created, and the more the rich learn to dodge these taxes. The recent slight rise in Chart 8-1 since the early 1990s is due to the rich getting richer and paying higher marginal tax rates.

Therefore, the other truth about taxes is that they aren't getting simpler and they aren't likely to near term. There have been increasing proposals for flat taxes and a simplified tax code. But in this era, much as in the early 1900s and Roaring '20s, when the rich are getting richer and the poor are getting poorer, most flat tax schemes would benefit the rich. And that simply is not politically feasible in a democratic system that is dominated by the average voter. Hence, the tax laws are getting still more complicated for targeting the more affluent and shielding the everyday citizen. Airline fares are so complicated that the agents at the airlines often can't figure them out, for the same reason. They have to discriminate between business and affluent passengers who will pay more and occasional tourists who won't.

Since we can't reasonably expect the tax code to get simpler until some miracle happens, above-average-income households will neces-

8-1. Federal Taxes as a Percentage of GDP

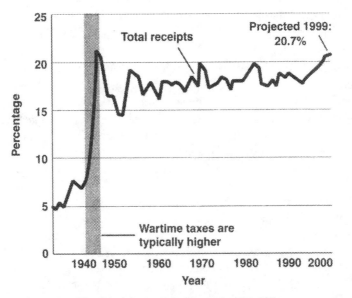

Data: Office of Management and Budget, Congressional Budget Office.

sarily have to pay attention to the impact of taxes on their wealth-building process. Not to criminally avoid taxes but to keep them at a reasonable rate, given the very high tax burden faced and the complexity of the system. Tax laws are constantly changing, and there is much confusion and misinformation about how you can legitimately reduce or defer taxes for leveraging your wealth-building process. There are 9,471 pages in the Internal Revenue Code, as compared to only 1,291 in the Bible. I will try to clear up most of this confusion in this chapter. But let me start with the simplest and most powerful principle for you to consider in tax strategies for investing.

> **The real benefit does not come merely from how much you save overall in one tax strategy versus another. The leverage comes from your ability to compound the investment returns over time on any tax savings or deferrals. That leverage can be enormous over decades, especially in the decade ahead, when we will see the highest potential investment returns.**

Let me give a quick example using the simple law of "72." If you take the average percentage of annual investment return you have or can expect to achieve, given the risks you are willing to take, and divide it into 72, it will show you approximately how often your money doubles in value. At the more typical long-term rate of return on stocks of around 11% to 12%, you will double your money every 6 to 6½ years. A 12% return is calculated by dividing 12 into 72, which gives you 6. That means if you save or defer $1 of taxes today, it will be worth $2 in 6 years, $4 in 12 years, $8 in 18 years, $16 in 24 years, and $32 in 30 years. Thirty years is a good time horizon for many of us, as the typical baby boomer is about 40 today and will want to retire perhaps around age 70.

Therefore, the real long-term benefit of a savings in taxes today is typically 32 times if you invest that money systematically until you begin retirement. Even if you are just deferring taxes for 30 years, you could pay those taxes then and have $31 left for every $1 you deferred when you start to retire. And the reality is that you aren't likely to spend all of that money immediately upon retirement but will be able to compound the effects for many more years. In 36 years that $1 deferral will be worth 64 times, and in 42 years, 128 times, and so on.

For the next decade I have shown that it is more reasonable to as
sume that you will receive investment returns of 17% to 18% at the
moderate risk level of the S&P 500. Or as high as 20%-plus at moderate risks by investing in the best sectors in a diversified manner (refer
back to Chapter 2). At those rates the compounding effect of tax savings is astonishing. At 18% you double your money every 4 years; at
24% you double every 3 years. Therefore, for every $1 in tax savings or
deferral today, at an 18% rate of return, you can create $4 of benefits
in 8 years or almost $6 in 10 years. At 24%, $1 today would be worth
$8 in 9 years, near the top of this boom. Hence, the compounding ef-
fect is very substantial just over the next decade in this type of stock
market.

It is very important that you start thinking this way. The more income and wealth you have, the higher your tax bracket and the more
you will appreciate what a competent financial advisor who under-
stands insurance and taxes as well as investments can do for you. Tax
strategies bring the most complex dimension to financial planning.
This means that your advisor must have competence in investment,
insurance, and tax and estate planning if you are a relatively high-
income or net-worth investor—or more important, if you are planning
to be. As the costs of investment transactions go down, the fees we
used to pay in the past for brokerage can go for integrated advice that
creates huge benefits in building and preserving wealth—not merely
for discount brokerage. That is why I don't see the role of the financial
advisor fading except in the simplest investment plans where tax consequences are minimal. And a higher percentage of people are going
to continue to move into the over-$250,000 investment levels that can
increasingly benefit from such integrated strategies.

Before you believe the popular notion that most of us are going to
be making our own investment decisions over the Internet, seriously
consider your investment potential and most seriously consider the tax
impacts of your investment decisions. Instead, consider how you can
find a competent financial advisor, as I outlined in Chapter 7, and
how you can interact with that advisor most efficiently over the Internet. In this chapter I am going to cover the key issues you have to consider in your own tax planning or in working with an advisor.

It's not that you should have to fully consider or figure out all the
points I will make in this chapter, but you should understand the types

of decisions you will have to make with an advisor and the impact those decisions could have. Again, they can be enormous. You typically have to take exponentially higher risks to increase your investment returns, but tax strategies can leverage those returns dramatically with little or no increase in your risks. It will often cost you a very small percentage of your assets. That could be the greatest investment you make if you understand the basic concepts in this chapter.

Tax Strategies for Creating Wealth

I am going to start with the simplest strategies for everyday and above-average-income investors for using tax strategies to create wealth beyond their investment returns. In the last part of this chapter, I will give an overview of strategies for very-high-net-worth investors for preserving their wealth and handing it down to future generations or charitable causes. I am not an expert in this field, but I work with many of the best financial advisors and have consulted with three of the experts I know, financial advisors who combine an extensive knowledge of investments, insurance, and taxes. These advisors include Bill Nelson, an independent financial planner in Dayton, Ohio; Joe Clark, an independent financial advisor in Anderson, Indiana; and Stephen Takeda, with Salomon Smith Barney in Orange County, California. They work with a full range of investors, not just the very wealthy. Steve's specialization focuses more on corporate and entrepreneurial executives.

Obviously, the first priority is to maximize your ability to defer income taxes through the variety of tax incentives provided through 401K plans at your company, especially if there are matching contributions from your employer. Or through IRAs that allow you to create your own retirement plan from your employment income. Or the new Roth IRAs that allow you to contribute to your own plan after paying taxes on that portion of your income, unlike a 401K plan. Or through SEP and Keogh plans for self-employed individuals and through deferred compensation plans like stock options and vested incentive plans for entrepreneurs and corporate executives.

These incentive plans have restrictions on how much of your income can be allocated to them, and these options are well known and covered in many investment books. Therefore, I am not going to spend much time on them. But it is important to note that many of these plans offer the greatest tax benefits because the portion of your income that goes into them is not taxed before it goes into your investment or retirement plan. That gives you a 20% to 45% advantage right off the bat, so you have much more to invest from the beginning. And then the income from those investments is compounded tax free until you withdraw it. It doesn't get better than this unless you can establish your own business as a public or private foundation, which I will cover later in this chapter.

Therefore, maximize your participation and contributions to these plans first. Go out of your way to do this. If you are not clear on these options and your ability to participate, talk to a financial advisor or a resource person at your company. Make sure that you have the same systematic investment strategy that I outlined in Chapter 2 to the degree possible with the funds and investment options offered by your company or plan. Too many people trade these accounts excessively or play it safe by choosing low-risk money market or bond funds when a prudent equity portfolio could produce much higher returns at similar or slightly higher risk levels. Since these plans represent a long-term investment horizon, even more conservative investors can prudently take higher risks and ride out the short-term volatility of the markets to their great benefit. For the next decade you want to focus on large cap growth and diversified international funds. And invest in technology, financial services, and health care funds if possible, or growth funds that heavily focus on these sectors.

It is also important to know that when you leave your company's 401K plan, you have 60 days to "roll it over" into a new plan that can maintain the tax-free investing benefits until you retire or withdraw income. If you fail to do this, you lose these cherished tax advantages and the incredible compounding effect into the future. Make sure to contact an investment professional or an investment firm that specializes in this to handle your transition to your best advantage immediately after changing jobs or retiring! An additional advantage here is that you can switch to a better investment portfolio with more options in mutual funds and investments than were in your past employer's plan. Hence, you can better leverage the strategies I outlined in Chapter 2. So evaluate the firms that offer 401K roll-over plans accordingly. Don't hand over your account to just anyone.

Having said the obvious first, I am going to start with a less-understood concept, variable annuities and variable universal life. These life-insurance-related investment vehicles allow you to defer taxes on investment income outside such common tax-deferral plans as 401Ks and IRAs. These investment vehicles have received a lot of bashing by academics and the press, especially since the capital gains tax rate was lowered to 20% in 1998. But this bashing represents more misinformation than truth. Are most of these people high-net-worth investors or highly qualified real-life advisors? Would you trust them to invest your money? Then why listen to them exclusively? They can be informative at times but are often motivated by a need for headlines that create controversial stories.

These stories typically go along these lines. Financial advisors are selling a lot of variable annuity products under the popular theme that it will save or defer taxes. Since everyone wants to avoid taxes, people buy these products even though their costs are high and they can't always benefit fully from the tax advantages. These advisors often make higher fees or commissions, and that's the only reason they peddle these "crummy" investment products! Have you heard this story in the last year or two?

My reality question to you is this: How come variable annuity sales are growing at very high rates, even after the changes in capital gains rates? And how come the most sophisticated investors and advisors have and still tend to use them? It would be one thing if this growth trend was being driven primarily by young, unsophisticated advisors accosting little old ladies, but that is not typically the case. And these hypothetical scenarios assume that you will have returns in the 8% or 10% range, which is not in tune with the reality of 17%-plus returns in this bull market. Tax-deferral benefits grow exponentially with your investment returns.

Let me start by acknowledging the appropriate part of this argument. Many investors are sold variable annuities that are not necessarily appropriate for them at slightly higher expenses and commissions. That is why I went into such depth in Chapter 7 to discuss how to find a competent advisor. There are scoundrels in this profession who care more about their commissions than their clients' performance and benefits. There are many more who mean well but don't have the tax expertise to properly evaluate the costs and benefits of such tax and investment vehicles. But if you find an advisor who does, I think you may well benefit from using variable annuities to deter taxes for decades and possibly forever.

Variable Annuities

Let me first define what a variable annuity is. First you need to understand the basics of life insurance. When you purchase a life insurance policy, you make payments that are then invested, net of the minor insurance or mortality costs and the investment management costs, tax free in a growing investment account that pays you a guaranteed death benefit when you die. This death benefit passes to your heirs or designated beneficiaries tax free if structured and titled properly. So, make sure you have a competent advisor. Insurance companies can guarantee this benefit to you even though they don't know when you will die, because they can leverage the same law of averages that I use to project key economic trends. In other words, they can pool your policy with large numbers of people and calculate precisely the life expectancy of that pool of people.

Some of you may be familiar with fixed annuities. These are contracts that invest the cash value of the money you give them—less the cost of the actuarial or mortality costs of pooling your life expectancy risks with other people and the administration expenses of investment—in long-term bonds or fixed-income investments. Insurance companies can lock in returns by purchasing long-term bonds at a fixed price and a fixed return. Instead of a death benefit, they pay you an income, starting now or at a future point when you determine you will need it, from the expected investment returns over the rest of your life, based on your estimated life expectancy.

That's why there are minor actuarial costs, just as with an insurance policy. You may live longer or not as long as expected. The insurance companies take that risk and average it over many people so that they can guarantee your payments despite variations in the actual number of years you will live. The longer you defer taking your income payments, the more the investment proceeds can grow and compound, allowing you to receive higher payments over a shorter life expectancy.

Many people find that the benefits of securing a guaranteed income over their lives outweigh the slight extra costs from the actuarial or insurance process. That's why life insurance has grown to be a major service industry in modern times. Life insurance actuaries were perhaps the first people to understand the predictable consequences of demographic trends. They were the first people I found who could accurately predict the future of human events.

Variable annuities have the same structure, except that they invest in equities, typically through mutual funds or in a combination of equity funds and fixed-income investments, which are not as predictable in their returns over time. That is why they are called "variable." Your payments over your life will be higher or lower depending on the actual investment returns achieved. But since equities typically generate higher returns than bonds, your payments will tend to be higher. I have gone out of my way to show why I think that equities will generate much higher returns than bonds over the coming decade. That's why variable annuities are so much more attractive and one reason they are growing so rapidly. As with fixed annuities, there are minor fees for investment management, just as there are in a mutual fund.

But one of the secrets that most people don't know is that the investment management fees tend to be a bit lower than for the same mutual fund you would invest in, because the insurance company doesn't have to pay the same marketing fees a mutual fund pays. You are getting what would be called an institutional rate or wholesale rate for marketing costs rather than a retail rate. Typically, the overall management fees for a mutual fund are around 0.95%, versus around 0.60% for a variable annuity. So there is a tangible savings that partially offsets the higher overall fees you pay for a variable annuity in actuarial costs and advisory costs. Note that these products are more complex and take more expertise to represent to investors. Hence, they should warrant a slightly higher advisory fee over a load mutual fund. A no-load fund is always less expensive, but you forgo the financial-planning process that can add much value to your wealth-building strategies. It is not fair to compare the returns of a load and a no-load fund. If you feel qualified to make your own investment decisions, then the up-front savings on a no-load fund should be credited to your time rather than to the fund.

The actuarial or insurance company costs more than offset the lower management fees, but the benefits of adapting payments to your life expectancy has a benefit. Variable annuities also have a life insurance benefit that guarantees that you receive your full investment if you die, even if the cash or investment value of your account is substantially less at that time. That is worth something. Overall, expect that the total cost, adjusting for lower investment management fees, will be about 0.30% to 0.50% per year higher for a variable annuity than for a mutual fund bought from an advisor. So the real question is this: What do you get for that slightly higher cost?

The standard answer is that you get the power of tax deferral and the ability to compound those deferred taxes at your investment returns and double that extra money every three to six years, depending on your expected investment returns described above. That is what makes variable (or fixed) annuities attractive to most people. Everyone likes to defer taxes and compound the difference over time. That is an easy sell.

But there is the growing counterargument today. Since capital gains taxes were reduced to 20% for an investment held 12 months or longer in 1998, many experts are saying that you are better off simply investing in stocks or an index fund and holding them over the time period you are investing for retirement. Or for when you anticipate needing income. By doing this, you can defer most or all of the taxes until you sell that investment and then pay a maximum of 20% versus as high as 40% in ordinary income taxes at the federal level. In other words, you don't pay taxes until you sell, so you just hold those stocks or a tax-efficient mutual fund until you need the money and you get the same tax-deferral benefits as a variable annuity. In addition, you pay lower capital gains rates instead of higher ordinary-income tax rates as you would in a variable (or fixed) annuity when you withdraw income. That is the one disadvantage of a variable annuity (although there are variations, called variable universal life, that can be structured for tax-free income withdrawals, as I will explain in a later section).

There are some real-life problems with that argument. And my approach has never been academic, nor has that of the best financial advisors I have worked with. They work through the real numbers in your situation and determine what the best strategy is likely to be. They don't consider hypothetical scenarios in a perfect world of rational investors who never let emotions affect their decisions and never change their plans, investment strategies, or income needs. Or where there are no transaction costs. That complicates a theoretical scenario. Hence, they take out these human factors to simplify their analysis.

Even index funds create some tax liability, as these funds have to sell stocks to meet the demand for withdrawals by investors, and they have to update the index for new stocks that enter and old stocks that exit. Hence, there will be some minor taxes that you pay as you go along, which you wouldn't in a variable annuity. In addition, most mutual funds have to hold a slightly higher amount of cash that isn't actively invested to meet these random demands for withdrawals by investors who want to sell when the markets are down. Therefore, the typical variable annuity, which experiences more systematic withdrawals, earns an estimated 0.25% more per year than a typical mutual fund. This is another factor that offsets the insurance and actuarial costs.

If you take the most tax-efficient strategy for capital gains benefits by investing in individual stocks to create total tax deferral instead of investing in mutual funds, then you have to hold those stocks for the entire period before you withdraw income to create the same tax-deferral effect as a variable annuity. How many of us will do that as such stocks fluctuate up and down or as even very large companies appear to gain or lose their competitive position over time? Every time you sell a stock or a mutual fund to switch to a better one, you will have to pay at least capital gains taxes, which will reduce the money you can continue to compound over time. And when you pay taxes, whether in minor amounts over time or when you finally withdraw the money for income, you will have to pay state and local taxes in addition to federal. And here the capital gains advantage does not apply. If your state taxes are 9% in California, then you will have to pay 20% federal taxes at the capital gains rate and 9% state taxes, or 29% in total, not the 20% assumed in many theoretical scenarios. Many states have lower tax rates, but the average of state and local would probably be about 5%, or after the deduction against federal taxes, 3% to 4%. So you are really paying something like 24% in taxes, even at capital gains rates.

Finally, investing in mutual funds without protection from taxation can occasionally cause a phenomenon called "phantom capital gains." If a mutual fund manager elects to sell stocks or securities that they have held before you got into the fund, then those capital gains, whether short- or long-term will be distributed to the present shareholders, which includes you. This means that you could occasionally pay taxes even in a year when your fund was down! This will not occur if your mutual fund investments are within a variable annuity.

The Real Secret to Variable Annuities

The greatest advantage to variable annuities comes from the most central investment strategy in this book. Since economic and investment cycles vary incredibly over time in a largely predictable manner, you simply can't have an effective investment strategy by holding any one stock, mutual fund, or portfolio of investments over the rest of your lifetime. If you invest in high-quality blue-chip stocks or large cap mutual funds today, the Dow could run up to 35,000 to 40,000 by 2008 and your investments could be worth three to four times what they are today. But then the Dow could fall back to 10,000 to 15,000 by 2020 or 2022 in the next extended down cycle, and you would lose most or all of your gains just when you may most need income for retirement.

To continue to expand your wealth in such a down economy, you will have to shift to bonds, international equities, and ultimately small cap stocks, as I outlined in Chapter 2. And then around 2020 to 2024 you will need to shift back into large cap stocks and new long-term equity strategies.

> **The insight here is very simple and very clear. If you are going to take advantage of the powerful investment strategies in this book, you will need to make major changes in your investment portfolio every 12 to 14 years or so. Every time you make such a shift, you will have to pay taxes on your gains, which will reduce the assets in your portfolio. A variable annuity allows you to make such shifts, both short-term and long-term, without any tax consequences.**

Hence, you can compound more of your investment assets over your lifetime and beat a tax-efficient strategy based on capital gains tax rates. You can have greater control over your investment portfolio to optimize your returns from systematic rebalancing. This can make variable annuities more attractive even for investors who aren't in the very highest tax brackets, especially if you expect your tax bracket to increase over time, as will occur for most of us. The long-term benefits here can be substantial. But even the short-term benefits giving you or your advisor the freedom to switch to better funds or sectors to optimize your returns without tax consequences can make a large difference over time. What variable annuities give you is the advantage of investing in high-performance mutual funds or index funds, allowing you to shift your strategy over time and rebalance your portfolio in the many ways I described in Chapter 2 without paying taxes until you need the money. When you finally do withdraw money for income and living needs, then the disadvantage is that you will have to pay higher ordinary-income rates. But it is also likely that you will be in a lower tax bracket in your retirement years, so the disadvantage will be less.

In summary, the key advantage is that you can control your investment strategies and defer taxes to a greater degree within a variable annuity investment. That is why the wealthiest investors and the best financial advisors still tend to prefer this investment vehicle. But you should examine the benefits with a qualified financial advisor and understand the disadvantages, including penalties for canceling or withdrawing income prematurely.

Variable Universal Life—The Best of All Worlds

There is a variation on variable annuities, called variable universal life, that allows you to invest in a life insurance policy that can defer taxes until your death or beyond. But it still allows you to withdraw income over your lifetime as needed into retirement **tax free!** If it is structured properly, you can withdraw nearly all of the investment value of the life insurance policy for your own use tax free. Here you invest in a life insurance policy that pays guaranteed death benefits to your designated beneficiaries. That means that such benefits may pass to your heirs or beneficiaries tax free, without estate taxes, as with any life insurance policy. The cash and growing investments of such a policy that you contribute to immediately or over time are invested like a variable annuity in equity mutual funds and/or fixed income, as you or your advisor choose. That means the higher potential returns from such equity-based investment strategies can increase the death benefit as the returns are invested, tax free, to increase your insurance policy.

But here is the unique feature of this investment vehicle. You can borrow from the cash or investment value of the portfolio inside the policy as you project you need money or income over time. That transaction is not considered a taxable event by the IRS. When you need income, the insurance company moves only that portion out of your higher-return equity investment accounts into a fixed-income account, creating predictable returns so that you can borrow against it. Here they act like a bank and lend you money against a predictable investment asset that is used as collateral. The practical reality is that you can withdraw almost all of your investment account over time as long as you leave a tiny portion to cover the actuarial or insurance costs of the life insurance policy. This means that you can effectively withdraw over 90% of the investment value that is growing over time at high equity rates of returns tax free. Or you can leave as much as you want to your heirs or beneficiaries. The best of choices for tax-free effects either way!

I don't want to get too far into the details here, as they can get rather complex and that is why you need a competent financial advisor to explore your options. But more insurance companies are offering to lend you that money at the same rate they are earning. That is called a "zero spread" loan. Some still charge you more interest than you are earning, as much as 2 percentage points or higher, but that is still cheaper than most bank loans you could obtain against such an asset. In that case there is another cost to calculate in. But if you can borrow at the same rate you are earning, then you are not depleting your assets except by the amount you withdraw and you can withdraw that income tax free. The money you don't set aside in a fixed-income account and borrow against for income continues to compound tax free within the variable life investment vehicle for as long as you keep it there.

With this vehicle you can defer taxes on income you don't need over your life and then withdraw it tax free rather than paying capital gains or ordinary-income tax rates through this loan clause. When you die, the loan balance is offset against your death benefit with no tax consequences. Whatever is left passes tax free to your heirs or designated beneficiaries. This is obviously the ultimate tax-deferral strategy.

But the catch is this: If you cancel the policy and don't keep it in force until your death, the life insurance advantage will revert and you will pay huge penalties because all of the investment income over the lifetime of the policy will have to be declared as ordinary income for tax purposes. But if you and your advisor understand and work this investment vehicle according to the rules, which allows you to withdraw almost all of the assets through loans, then it can be incredibly effective and tax efficient. And there is no reason you should have to cancel it, even if you need income. Just make sure you don't naively cancel it! Here, again, you pay a little extra for the life insurance and estate tax benefits, but that obviously can be well worth it.

If you do choose to leave substantial benefits to your heirs, those benefits will escape taxes in your estate, which can be as high as 55%. And that income will be received tax free. The only limitation is that your beneficiaries will be taxed on any investment returns they receive on that money from that point on unless you use creative strategies to avoid that, as I will cover later in this chapter. Here again, I want to warn you that these strategies are often complex and you should make sure you are dealing with a competent advisor who can evaluate the costs and benefits and set them up properly.

The Three Buckets

Bill Nelson has a simple way of looking at your tax strategies and how to withdraw income from them over your lifetime, which he calls the three buckets. There are three types of tax strategies or investment vehicles. They produce one of the following income streams for tax purposes:

1. Tax-free income
2. Taxable income
3. Tax-deferred income

Tax-free income includes state and municipal bonds that are not taxed at the federal level and sometimes not taxed at the state or local level. These investment vehicles offer lower rates of return and typically are marginally attractive only for the highest-tax-bracket investors who wish to be in fixed-income investments. Again, I see fixed income as a poor investment class for most investors in the coming decade of very high equity returns at often very reasonable risks.

Taxable investments include dividends from stocks and mutual funds; interest from bonds and preferred stocks; and gains from the sale of stocks or mutual funds. Tax-deferred investments include variable annuities, 401K plans, IRAs, SEPs, Keoghs, and qualified stock options and deferred-compensation plans. Your investment strategy may include some or all of these investment vehicles. The important point to understand is that when you withdraw income for retirement or other needs, you want to use these vehicles in that descending order to maximize your wealth-building process.

For tax-free income, or bucket #1, spend that money first because you aren't taxed at all or penalized for using that income. This should be obvious, but it is also easy to overlook if you aren't "tax-conscious." For taxable income, or bucket #2, you are better to leave it invested until you need the income and then pay lower capital gains tax rates when you do sell the investment and spend the money. Take money out of a tax-deferred account, or bucket #3, last because it can continue to grow at compound rates and you have to pay the highest ordinary-income tax rates when you withdraw it. However, you must take into account the minimal withdrawals you must make from some of these investment vehicles at certain ages as required by tax laws. Again, here is where you have to do your homework or use an advisor.

If you receive forced income from a tax-free municipal bond, from dividends, or a mutual fund distribution of capital gains that you don't need for current income, reinvest it in a tax-free or a tax-deferred vehicle. Let's say you have a variable annuity that is tax deferred and a variable universal life policy that you can withdraw income from tax free by borrowing against the value of the life insurance policy. Then withdraw the tax-free income from the variable life vehicle first and keep the tax deferrals going for the variable annuity, as you will have to pay ordinary-income tax rates if you withdraw from it.

Preserving Your Wealth Through Tax-Based Investment Strategies

For investors who have or may foresee having a net worth of $1 million or more, estate taxes and the ability to preserve your wealth for your kids or their kids or for charitable causes you value becomes critical. Given this incredible boom and increasing access to 401K and pension plans, far more of us are going to become millionaires in our lifetime. Here is where the greatest complexity and advantages from financial planning come into play. As sophisticated as many wealthy people can be, almost as many overlook these critical estate-planning issues, largely because they have created and managed their own wealth on their own. They naturally think, "I have managed this on my own, and I have done well. Therefore I don't need help in financial planning. My own success has demonstrated that I don't need financial-planning advice. I am a self-made person." This syndrome is more typical than you might think for the "millionaire next door."

My advice to you, if you fall into this increasing category, is to focus on what you do best and to delegate the more specialized aspects of investment management and estate and tax planning to an expert who can leverage your wealth-building capacities and lifestyle opportunities to an even greater degree. Don't be penny-wise and pound-foolish!

Many of us simply don't want to think about our death and its effect on our families and heirs or on society when we consider the options for charitable giving, which I will cover briefly. Estate taxes represent the greatest of all tax penalties. Your estate is exempt of taxes on $650,000 in assets, rising up to $1,000,000 by 2002. Above that, your estate will be taxed at up to 55%. Each spouse can create a trust, called an AB credit shelter, which creates two separate estates. This doubles a married couple's effective exemption up to $2,000,000 by 2002. Again, this is a complex field of tax law. I just want to alert you to the penalties you need to consider with a financial advisor or tax expert to make the right decisions. A whole book could be written on this subject alone, and I am not foremost a tax expert.

Using Gifting to Pass Your Assets Tax Free

One of the best-known ways to pass your assets to your heirs is to give up to $10,000 per year to each family member or heir tax free. This amount can come from each spouse, which doubles the gifting to $20,000 per family member or heir. If you are married and have three children, you can give each $20,000 per year, for a total of $60,000 per year that will avoid estate taxes and be received tax free by your kids. You can also give the same amount to each of their kids and so on. If you have the cash flow and plan far enough ahead, you can avoid much in estate taxes through this simple strategy. When there are market corrections, you can give stocks or investments at lower valuations and increase your giving power.

Using Life Insurance and Variable Universal Life to Avoid Estate Taxes

As I have already mentioned, you can purchase life insurance through a fixed payment or a series of payments or invest in a variable universal life policy to use the power of higher-return equity investments to create a growing death benefit that will pass to your heirs tax free. But make sure to title them properly to your heirs through a trust to avoid estate taxes.

Using Life Insurance Trusts to Distribute Income over Your Heirs' Lifetime

One of the biggest problems high-net-worth families and individuals face is how to transfer assets or income from your assets to your kids or heirs without spoiling them or having them just blow the money in ways that you wouldn't intend or that aren't in their best interests. One study by the American Banking Association found that the average inheritance is spent within 17 months! The statistics would surely not be that extreme for large inheritances—we are talking about the average here. But the point is powerful. A sudden inheritance can cause even the best people to abandon their long-term perspective and just live it up or buy all the things they've always wanted to reduce the present stress of living.

The best way to give money to people you love is to give it to them over time or to give it for specific uses that are beneficial, like their education or their kids' education or starting a business or investing in a house or real estate. To give your kids the message that they can have enough income to do anything they want can be detrimental unless they are very mature or self-actualized. It can also be very beneficial to include written investment policies that ensure that the money passed over time to your heirs is invested soundly or in accordance with the long-term strategies in this book. Sudden inheritances can be squandered not only through sudden expenditures but also through poor investment strategies or through bad advice from inexperienced advisors. This is where insurance-funded trusts can be very beneficial.

You can have your death benefits from a life insurance policy or a variable universal life policy pass to your heirs through a trust that pays them an income from the continued tax-free compounding of investment proceeds of the policy over time. Such a trust can also stipulate the purposes for which the proceeds can be used and the investment strategies to be followed. This obviously gives you far more control over how and when the proceeds are used.

The way this is typically accomplished is through an irrevocable life insurance trust based on a "second to die" benefit. That means that the death benefit passes into a trust for the benefit of your heirs only when the second spouse or both of you die if you are married. The trust needs to be managed by what is called a "friendly trustee." That means someone who has the best interests of your heir at heart and not the fees that could accrue from continuing to manage the investments.

Obviously, an investment management company or trust department would benefit from distributing as little as possible to your heirs and keeping the assets in the trust high and the management and administration fees high. On the other hand, if you designate a family member to oversee the trust, then you put a great responsibility on that person, and all the other family members or beneficiaries will be pressuring that person to give them what they want.

Hence, the best method may be to designate a trusted financial advisor or lawyer to administer the trust according to very carefully designated policies that you create with them in advance. These policies should designate how the money is distributed over what time frames and for what needs and how the assets of the trust will be invested. The investment value of the trust can be structured to continue to grow tax free until distributed according to your policies. You can also create generation-skipping trusts that accumulate and pass tax free to future generations along the same guidelines. The compounded returns of such very-long-term trusts can allow you to use the very-long-term investment cycles and strategies outlined in this book to create extraordinary wealth for many generations to come. And to have that wealth allocated to very prudent uses and not to the worst natural human tendencies, which can gravitate toward short-term indulgences and complacency. Most of us would rather see our kids continue to grow and learn and advance in their achievements and contributions to society rather than partying the rest of their lives or simply losing the motivation to grow and contribute more.

Extending the Tax-Deferral Benefits of IRAs to Your Heirs

Most people don't understand that you can pass the tax-deferred returns on your IRA accounts partially to your heirs. These tax-deferred vehicles impose penalties of 10% if you pull out income before age $59\frac{1}{2}$. And they force distributions of the assets in such a plan after age $70\frac{1}{2}$. In other words, if you are going to enjoy the tax benefits of doing what society wants you to do to provide for your retirement without becoming a burden on our government, then you have to use these tax-incentive plans for your retirement. From age $70\frac{1}{2}$ on, you are required to withdraw the percentage of your assets in your IRA at an annual rate that is commensurate to pay out your assets over your life expectancy.

For example, if your life expectancy at age $70\frac{1}{2}$ is 16 years, then you would have to withdraw $\frac{1}{16}$ of your assets in your IRA per year and pay ordinary income tax on those withdrawals. But you can defer that further by using a trust to convey your retirement plan partially or fully to a beneficiary, like your spouse, your kids, or a friend. Then their life expectancy will be used on that portion to reduce the required withdrawals and taxable income. For example, if your life expectancy is 16 years but your child's is 40 years, then the retirement plan would have to distribute income and benefits to your child at only $\frac{1}{40}$ of the assets per year instead of $\frac{1}{16}$. This would allow your retirement plan to defer taxes and accumulate investment returns much longer. This would obviously be possible only to the degree that you didn't need the income for your own retirement needs. If you receive a lump-sum distribution from your 401K plan, then you can roll it over into your IRA and then accomplish the same effects through such an IRA beneficiary trust.

Setting Up Charitable Remainder Trusts

There is another option for maximizing your wealth for benefiting causes that you value beyond the needs you have for retirement and that you determine are optimal for supporting your kids' or heirs' needs without spoiling them. The first such option comes from charitable remainder trusts. You can donate assets to a trust that is designated to go to the IRS-approved charity of your choice upon your death. Such a trust can invest the proceeds in fixed income or equities/mutual funds to generate a growing value over the rest of your lifetime. That trust can in turn pay you a fixed income over your life. That income to you will be taxable as ordinary income when you receive it, and you can also give a fixed income to the charity if you desire. But the assets that remain in the trust when you die will be given to the charity. Here again, you can use the power of compounding tax-free returns to grow your assets and take income only as you anticipate needing it over time. You pay taxes only when you finally take the income. In addition, you receive a tax deduction for the estimated value today of that gifted asset based on the future value discounting for the time value of money. That tax deduction can save you money today that can be invested for the future and compounded.

The results can be very powerful. Often you can pay yourself an income close to, or as good as, the income you would have received from investing the money yourself and paying taxes on those returns. And you do this while giving as much or more than you would have been able to give to the charity at the point you set up such a trust. That is a win-win strategy for both you and the charity you value. Why does the government allow this at its expense in tax revenues? Because it wants to support charitable causes that it would have to allocate revenues to for the good of society.

The power for you is that you can direct tax-deferred money toward the causes that you value most rather than what the general voting population dictates. Therefore, I strongly recommend that you consider this option with a competent financial advisor, especially if you have a net worth or income beyond your needs for living into retirement or beyond the prudent needs for passing your assets and an income to your heirs responsibly.

Again, more and more people are realizing that passing too much wealth to their kids or passing it in an unstructured way can work more to their detriment than to their advantage. If they realize that they already have it made, will they be motivated to continue to learn and grow? Can you nurture your kids too much and provide too much for them without ensuring enough challenges that will force them to grow and to develop their own self-esteem and self-actualization?

Wealth rarely lasts more than a generation or two without being overexploited and creating excessive complacency and idle direction. History has proved this over and over again. But the security of self-esteem and wealth can also contribute to the highest evolution of self-actualization in your kids and heirs. There is an even better way to benefit the charitable causes of your choosing and to help your kids contribute to society in the highest potential of self-actualization.

The Ultimate Tax Strategy for Preserving Wealth and Contributing to Society: Charitable Foundations

As many of the most wealthy families have done over the past century, you can use your excess wealth to set up a private or public foundation while you are living or upon your death. Your kids or heirs can work for this foundation and further their and your contribution to society. Let me start with the ultimate lifestyle strategy here and work back. If what you do for a living is educational or potentially charitable in nature, then you can set up your profession today as a public foundation. The advantage is simple. The revenues from your activities can flow into this public foundation and escape income taxation from the outset, giving you the greatest tax-deferral benefits, like a 401K or an IRA plan. The investment income then compounds tax free over time, making this the ultimate tax-deferral vehicle.

You can draw an income up to the value of your services, but only to the extent you need that income to live on. That means the remainder of your income or revenues, less expenses, is not taxed to begin with, saving you as much as 30% to 45% off the bat. Then those proceeds can be invested and compounded tax free, which leverages your ability to expand the assets in the foundation. Then you can withdraw income for the rest of your life as needed from the tax-deferred income and investment returns, as long as you are serving the purposes of the foundation and those services qualify according to the tax laws.

The goals and purposes of the foundation can change over time as your or your heirs' perception of the most worthy causes changes over time. You can allow for more or less change in charitable recipients as you see fit. Public foundations have more restrictions on the percentage of contributions or income sources that can come from any one source and restrictions on the level of investment income that can be generated within it. Private foundations have fewer such restrictions but impose minimal taxes on investment income accumulated. They also impose greater restrictions on the tax-deductibility for donors. That is their disadvantage.

Setting up and administering your own foundation will require a certain amount in fees and the advice of a good lawyer and financial planner or tax consultant. But the benefits to you and society can be enormous. Even for people who don't have the level of income or resources that could justify the costs of such a legal entity, there are umbrella organizations like the Heritage Foundation. These IRS-approved charitable organizations can allow you to start your foundation at lower initial costs and then set up your own foundation when you grow to a level that would justify doing that. The disadvantage is simply that you do not control the umbrella organization that you join. Hence, you must make sure they have sound legal and administration policies and an unblemished track record of dealing with the smaller organizations they take in.

Summary

Let me give you one parting thought from Bruce Wright, a fellow speaker and author in the financial services industry: Don't enter into any business or long-term investment without a clear consideration of your entry and exit strategy. Why are you doing this? How much wealth is enough? How and when do you foresee exiting from this investment? And how do you need to structure this business or investment at the outset to accomplish your clear objectives? Too many of us make piecemeal decisions as we make investments and accumulate wealth.

It requires a comprehensive plan and the proper structuring and titling of your investments and wealth, including tax and estate planning, to make sure that you achieve your most cherished ideals and that your wealth goes to the people and causes you would prefer. You should also consider what really makes a difference to you and how you really want to spend your time, down to your daily calendar. Don't blindly make decisions that seem to make more money or extend your work. Consider what you would do if you had the financial freedom. That is what money is all about, and that is where the right knowledge and competent advisors can truly help you. Make sure you get there, and not just become the richest person in the graveyard.

Wealth is a natural stage in higher evolution, beyond survival, belonging, and even self-esteem. Few have achieved it in history; now many of us will to degrees never thought possible. It is about creating greater choice for yourself and those you love. It is a means to change the world for the better in whatever way you desire and are able. Consider today what you want to do for the rest of your life, and think about what creates the greatest inner satisfaction for you. Don't just become wealthy—make a difference, leave a legacy. My most summary insight is the following:

You can be rich within your own definition and lifestyle for the rest of your life in any economic scenario. Leverage the insights in this book to invest systematically in trends that can build your wealth, lifestyle, and influence. Find a competent planner

or mentor who can help you objectively evaluate your options, develop a long-term plan, and stick to it. And make sure you integrate all aspects of financial planning to maximize your wealth—from cash management and budgeting to credit and borrowing, from risk management and insurance to investment building and tax and estate planning. And then use it wisely to achieve your highest aspirations.

Don't let your ego get in the way of using a competent advisor who is more qualified and objective. But make sure to choose one who has those qualities and skills. Most important, don't let your valuable time or lack of specialized expertise get in the way of your lifestyle. You should be doing what you do best in this incredible boom and leveraging the time and talents of other specialists—both to enhance your wealth and to free up your time for enjoying life. Start today by reconsidering your life goals and by sitting down with someone who can help you systematically achieve those goals. Don't put off this consideration. By starting now, you allow every day to work for you rather than against you.

Best of success to you in the Roaring 2000s!

Products and Services from the H. S. Dent Foundation

For Corporations and Executives

Keynote Presentations
In-House Training Seminars
Business Consulting
Executive Strategy Sessions
H. S. Dent Forecast Newsletter
Quantity Discounts on Books and Materials

For Financial Advisors and Institutional Investors

Mutual Fund, Unit Investment Trust, Private Investment
*   Partnership*
Marketing and Seminar Systems
Audiotapes for Prospecting
H. S. Dent Forecast Newsletter
Desk and Wall Charts of the "Spending Wave"
Special Reports on the Markets and Financial Services Industry
Strategic Marketing Assessment

For Individuals and Investors

Mutual Fund, Unit Investment Trust, Private Investment
*   Partnership*
H. S. Dent Forecast Newsletter
H. S. Dent Internet Site . . . www.hsdent.com

Books
Videotapes
Audiotapes
Special Reports

Call Toll-Free Today: 1-800-371-9119
Or visit our Web site: www.hsdent.com

Index

About the Author

Harry S. Dent, Jr., president of H. S. Dent Advisors, is an investment strategist and economic futurist employed widely by the best financial advisors and their investment clients around the country. He is a sub-advisor to the AIM Dent Demographic Trends Fund, an actively managed mutual fund. He is a consultant to the Van Kampen Roaring 2000s Trust, a unit investment trust. He also manages a number of private funds. He is the author of *The Roaring 2000s* and *The Great Boom Ahead*. He is also president of the H. S. Dent Foundation, whose mission is simple: "helping people understand change." He graduated from Harvard Business School as a Baker Scholar.

What's on our economic horizon?
Find out what's happening
tomorrow today!

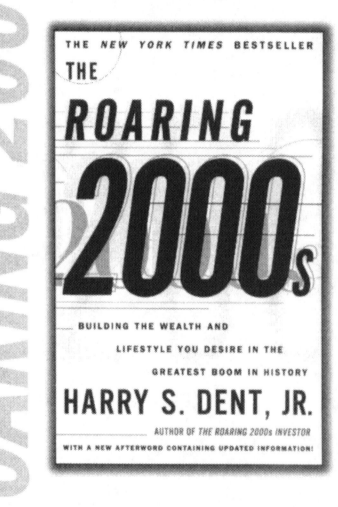

Printed in the United States
By Bookmasters